DAYTRIPPER

50 Trips In and Around Southwestern Ontario

Donna Gibbs Carpenter
Photographs by Dean Robinson

THE BOSTON MILLS PRESS

APPRECIATION

As with any worthwhile project, this book was really a collaborative effort. There are a few people whose support and assistance are especially appreciated. Liz Evans worked long and hard at the computer keyboard until I was ready to fly solo. My father, C. William Gibbs, is the best in-family editor anyone ever had. Griffin sat patiently in his car seat for many hours while Katie acted as map-reader and daytripper extraordinaire. My greatest debt of gratitude is owed to husband Stephen; it is only his natural unselfishness that prevents his name from being on the front cover.

CANADIAN CATALOGUING IN PUBLICATION DATA

Carpenter, Donna May Gibbs, 1954-
  Daytripper

ISBN 1-55046-038-2

1. Ontario — Description and travel — 1981-
Guide-books. I. Title.

FC3095.S68A3 1990   917.13'2044   C90-093881-1
F1059.S68C3 1990

Edited by Noel Hudson
Designed by Donna Gibbs Carpenter and Gill Stead
Cover Design by Gill Stead
Map Illustrations by Mary Firth
Typeset by Donna Gibbs Carpenter and Waterloo Printing, Waterloo
Printed by Ainsworth Press, Kitchener

COVER PHOTOGRAPH: The Little Inn, Bayfield

Published by:
THE BOSTON MILLS PRESS
132 Main Street
Erin, Ontario
N0B 1T0
(519) 833-2407

American Association
for State and Local History
Award of Merit

Winners of the
Heritage Canada
Communications Award

We wish to acknowledge the financial assistance and encouragement of The Canada Council, the Ontario Arts Council and the Office of the Secretary of State.

TABLE OF CONTENTS

INTRODUCTION   6
THE TRIP-FINDER   8
1. AMHERSTBURG (*All Quiet on the Western Front*)   10
2. WINDSOR (*Windsor Walkabout*)   12
3. WALKERVILLE (*The Town that Walker Built*)   14
4. HARROW (*A Harrowing Experience*)   16
5. KINGSVILLE (*Local Hero*)   18
6. LEAMINGTON (*Spitting Image*)   20
7. BLENHEIM (*Birdland*)   22
8. CHATHAM (*Follow the North Star*)   24
9. SARNIA (*Life on the River*)   26
10. PETROLIA (*Petrol Power*)   28
11. GRAND BEND (*The Alternative Grand Bend*)   30
12. BAYFIELD (*City Comforts/Country Charm*)   32
13. GODERICH (*Sunset Strip*)   34
14. BLYTH (*Blyth Spirit*)   36
15. LONDON (*A Walk on the Historic Side*)   38
16. LONDON (*A Day for the Kids*)   42
17. LONDON (*The Good Life*)   44
18. LONDON (*A Tale of Two Settlements*)   46
19. PORT STANLEY (*Port Stanley Revisited*)   48
20. SPARTA (*Sand in Your Shoes*)   50
21. ST. MARYS (*Stonetown*)   52
22. STRATFORD (*Much Ado About Something*)   56
23. INGERSOLL (*More Cheese, Please*)   58
24. NORWICH (*Flower Power*)   60
25. SIMCOE (*Tobacco Road*)   62
26. PORT DOVER (*Perch Awhile in Port Dover*)   64
27. BRANTFORD (*The Red Tile*)   66
28. CALEDONIA (*Deepest, Darkest Ontario*)   68
29. ST. GEORGE (*An Apple a Day*)   70
30. CAMBRIDGE (*Down by the Old Millstream*)   72
31. KITCHENER (*For Shoppers Only*)   76
32. WATERLOO (*A Fistful of Museums*)   78
33. ST. JACOBS (*To Market, To Market*)   80
34. ELORA (*Gorgeous Ontario*)   82
35. FERGUS (*The Scottish Connection*)   84
36. GUELPH (*Galleria Guelph*)   86
37. ROCKWOOD (*History in Motion*)   88
38. CAMPBELLVILLE (*Birds of a Feather*)   90
39. ANCASTER (*A Taste of the Past*)   92
40. DUNDAS (*Spring Thaw*)   94
41. HAMILTON (*Industrial Revolutions*)   98
42. BURLINGTON (*A Thing of Beauty is a Joy Forever*)   100
43. JORDAN (*Ontario, How Sweet It Is*)   102
44. PORT DALHOUSIE (*Spend a Day in Port*)   106
45. ST. CATHARINES (*Canal Route*)   108
46. NIAGARA-ON-THE-LAKE (*The Play's the Thing, But Not Everything*)   110
47. NIAGARA-ON-THE-LAKE (*1812 Overture*)   112
48. NIAGARA FALLS (*City of Light*)   114
49. NIAGARA FALLS (*Nature's Water Park*)   116
50. FORT ERIE (*From Fort to Port*)   118
BIBLIOGRAPHY   120

Evening in rural Ontario

INTRODUCTION

We are so fortunate to live in Ontario. Adventures of every description lie around each bend in the road. *Daytripper* will open your eyes to places worth discovering, even though they may have existed right under your nose for years.

What is a daytrip? It's an outing lasting anywhere from a few hours to a full day. That way you can have an interesting and invigorating holiday *and* sleep in your own bed. This also means that the trips described in *Daytripper* are within a convenient distance of home, cottage, work, family and friends. Although the trips in this book are designed to be a day's length, this doesn't mean that you can't string several of them together for a full holiday.

This volume of *Daytripper* covers southwestern Ontario. The western portion of the region is the market garden of the province, growing everything from apples to zucchini.

There are also hot bird-watching spots, forts ringing with musket fire, towns settled by fugitive slaves, and some of the best beaches anywhere. The eastern portion of the region is rich in picturesque stone villages, antique-hunting, world-class theatre, intriguing museums and mighty Niagara Falls.

The number of trips possible within southwestern Ontario is almost unlimited, but the best 50 have been carefully chosen. *Daytripper* has done the work of selecting the best natural and cultural features southwestern Ontario has to offer, and packages these as single-theme excursions. While each trip has a theme, it also includes several activities, so that each day is filled with variety. For example, a day spent visiting a fishing village may include walking, boating, and a museum visit. Each trip description includes recommendations for picnicking spots and restaurants.

Daytripper is suitable for senior citizens, families of all ages, and single travellers. While many trips include a good walk or other exercise, this is not a book of rugged activities, and any of the trips can be tailored to the needs of a senior or toddler. These trips have been child-tested; well-behaved children are welcome at all the sites mentioned.

Daytripper is not just for locals. It is also aimed at tourists looking for Ontario beyond its major attractions; it can be invaluable for showing off the province to visiting relatives and friends. Take it with you on business trips and to the cottage for things to do off-hours or on a rainy day.

There are a few things that daytrippers will not find in this book. Large, well-known attractions, such as amusement parks, will not be described. They are expensive and incompatible with the local culture and landscape. Most special events and festivals will not be described in *Daytripper*. The trips in this book are suitable over an extended season, not limited to only a week or two in the year. Any (pre-arranged) factory tours or other special-admission tours included in this book are those that are truly "visitor-friendly," since *Daytripper* adventures are meant to be spontaneous, without a great deal of advance planning.

HOW TO USE THIS BOOK

Keep it handy! You never know when you'll have a day free for an unplanned trip, so be prepared with *Daytripper* by the front door or in the glove compartment.

Make sure you have an up-to-date, good-quality road map. The standard Government of Ontario highway map is very good, and the directions described in *Daytripper* assume that you have a map of at least this detail.

Use the trip-finder on the following pages to find trips within a close drive of home, or to find trips relating to your particular hobby or interest.

The season and hours of operation for museums and other attractions sometimes change, so if a trip includes a site of special interest to you, avoid disappointment by phoning ahead to check on hours of operation. This is particularly good advice for holiday periods. Phone numbers have been provided for those restaurants where reservations are recommended, or where a particular restaurant is a key element in a trip. Please also phone ahead to check on wheelchair accessibility and other special needs.

Most museums and other attractions charge an admission fee. In almost all cases this is a very modest charge, considering the quality of the sites. You won't be disappointed. Some attractions, such as boat cruises, may cost a little more than a museum, but then they offer a longer outing. The restaurants and inns suggested for daytrippers are average or inexpensive in price, unless otherwise noted. Some of the more costly places may be within limited budgets at lunchtime.

Don't use *Daytripper* as the last word on adventuring. Use it as a beginning, and feel free to go off discovering on your own. Ask questions of people you meet—shop owners, waiters and waitresses, and fellow travellers. Ontarians are pleased to tell of the special places within their own area. Follow their suggestions.

Happy trails to you!

Donna Gibbs Carpenter

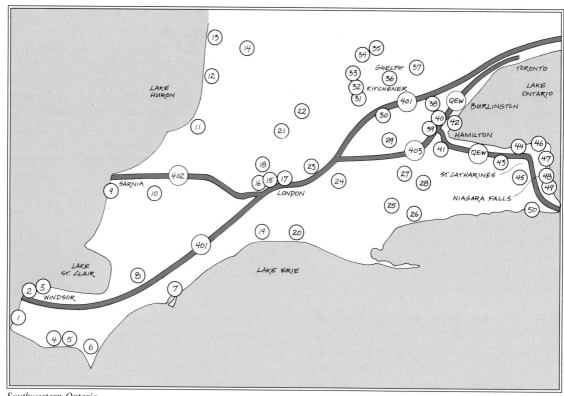

Southwestern Ontario

THE TRIP-FINDER

This trip-finder is an index to all 50 daytrips. It can be used in two ways. You can look up a topic of special interest and find the daytrip numbers listed. These numbers correspond to the number in large print at the beginning of each trip description. Or you can look up your home location and find the trips which are within a short distance (approximately 90 minutes) of home.

ACTIVITY TRIPS

HIKING, WALKING
1, 2, 6, 7, 11, 15, 17, 20, 21, 24, 30, 34, 35, 37, 38, 39, 40, 42, 43, 46, 48, 49

FISHING
6, 7, 9, 11, 18, 19, 26, 33, 34, 35, 37, 44, 50

BIKING
6, 7, 11, 13, 15, 16, 17, 21, 32, 35, 36, 37, 44, 45, 46, 47

WINTER SPORTS
6, 7, 11, 12, 15, 18, 33, 34, 38, 39, 40, 42, 48

PLEASURE DRIVING
1, 2, 9, 12, 14, 24, 28, 29, 33, 39, 43, 45, 48, 47, 49

SHOPPING
12, 14, 17, 19, 20, 21, 22, 23, 24, 26, 29, 30, 31, 33, 34, 35, 36, 44, 46

BOATING, CRUISES, BOAT-WATCHING
1, 2, 7, 9, 12, 13, 16, 19, 26, 28, 44, 45, 46, 49, 50

SWIMMING
5, 6, 7, 9, 11, 12, 13, 18, 19, 20, 21, 26, 34, 35, 37, 44, 45, 50

8

THEME TRIPS

HISTORY
1, 3, 5, 8, 10, 11, 13, 15, 17, 20, 21, 23, 25, 27, 30, 32, 35, 37, 39, 41, 44, 46, 47, 50

NATURE
2, 5, 6, 7, 11, 16, 24, 28, 32, 34, 37, 38, 39, 40, 42, 43, 49

GARDENS
2, 3, 16, 22, 24, 35, 40, 42, 43, 46, 48

THEATRE
14, 22, 46

INDUSTRY
3, 4, 10, 14, 23, 25, 30, 31, 32, 41, 43, 45

CULTURAL HERITAGE
1, 8, 27, 32, 33, 35

FARMING AND FARM MARKETS
2, 4, 18, 23, 25, 29, 30, 33, 35, 39, 43

ENGINEERING
9, 10, 21, 37, 41, 44, 45, 49, 50

VISUAL ARTS, CRAFTS
1, 12, 20, 22, 32, 36, 39, 42, 46

HISTORIC INNS
12, 19, 20, 21, 23, 29, 30, 33, 34, 35, 38, 39, 44, 46

TIMELY TRIPS

The following list suggests trips for those times when it can be difficult to find something to do.

WINTER
11, 15, 18, 21, 22, 23, 27, 30, 31, 32, 33, 34, 35, 36, 38, 39, 40, 41, 42, 44, 48

SUNDAY
1, 2, 6, 7, 8, 9, 10, 11, 12, 13, 14, 15, 16, 17, 19, 20, 22, 23, 26, 27, 29, 33, 34, 35, 36, 37, 38, 39, 41, 42, 45, 46, 47, 49, 50

RAINY DAYS
3, 23, 31, 32, 36, 41, 42

TRIPS BY LOCATION

This list indicates which trips are within about a 90-minute drive of the larger cities within southwestern Ontario and Festival Country. If you are a daytripper who likes to travel even further, then consult the preceeding map.

WINDSOR
1, 2, 3, 4, 5, 6, 7, 8, 9, 10

SARNIA
7, 8, 9, 10, 11, 12, 13, 14, 15, 16, 17, 18, 19, 23

LONDON
7, 8, 9, 10, 11, 12, 13, 14, 15, 16, 17, 18, 19, 20, 21, 22, 23, 24, 25, 26, 27, 28, 29, 30, 31, 32, 33, 34, 35, 36, 37, 38, 39, 40, 41

KITCHENER-WATERLOO
14, 15, 16, 17, 18, 19, 20, 21, 22, 23, 24, 25, 26, 27, 28, 29, 30, 31, 32, 33, 34, 35, 36, 37, 38, 39, 40, 41, 42, 43, 44, 45, 46, 47, 48, 49

GUELPH
15, 16, 17, 18, 21, 22, 23, 24, 25, 26, 27, 28, 29, 30, 31, 32, 33, 34, 35, 36, 37, 38, 39, 40, 41, 42, 43, 44, 45, 46, 47, 48, 49

HAMILTON, BURLINGTON
15, 16, 17, 18, 21, 23, 24, 26, 27, 28, 29, 30, 31, 32, 33, 34, 35, 36, 37, 38, 39, 40, 41, 42, 43, 44, 45, 46, 47, 48, 49, 50

ST. CATHARINES
25, 26, 27, 28, 29, 30, 31, 32, 33, 34, 35, 36, 37, 38, 39, 40, 41, 42, 43, 44, 45, 46, 47, 48, 49, 50

WESTERN TORONTO, MISSISSAUGA
22, 23, 24, 25, 26, 27, 28, 29, 30, 31, 32, 33, 34, 35, 36, 37, 38, 39, 40, 41, 42, 43, 44, 45, 46, 47, 48, 49, 50

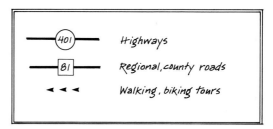

══●401●══	Highways
══▫81▫══	Regional, county roads
◄ ◄ ◄	Walking, biking tours

1 AMHERSTBURG
All Quiet on the Western Front

Amherstburg is only 20 minutes from the city of Windsor along scenic Highway 18, but it seems like another world. Uncrowded, historic, and with an unbeatable riverside setting, Amherstburg is an all-round daytrip offering something for everyone.

The first stop of the day must be Fort Malden, located on Laird Avenue and easily found by following street signs. The Amherstburg area saw European exploration and settlement in the mid-1700s, and in 1796 Fort Malden became the premier British frontier post. The advantages of the site in controlling river traffic are obvious. It also became a shipbuilding centre and the headquarters of the British Indian Department.

The fort has a checkered past. Originally a British headquarters during the War of 1812, and then occupied by Americans from 1813-1815, Fort Malden was returned to the British. Regular forces were withdrawn in 1836, only to have them return to engage in the Rebellion of 1837. Political stability returned to war-torn Essex, and the fort became a home for pensioned soldiers and later an asylum.

Although very little of the original fort remains to be seen — the 1840 earthworks, an 1819 barracks, and a pensioner's cottage — there's still a lot to be learned at Fort Malden. The visitor of today receives a thorough history of the fort. Museum exhibits review causes of the 1812 War, major battles, and illustrate the life of a typical officer and a humble infantryman. The barracks are the highlight of the fort, bringing history to life with authentic furnishings, costumed soldiers and cookhouse staff. Children may try on uniforms and pose with soldiers. There are special events daily, including musket firings, and in August a major military tattoo takes place. Four hectares of groomed parkland provide a perfect place to watch the ships on the busiest shipping channel in the world.

Just south of Fort Malden is the Park House Museum, the oldest house within 400 kilometres. The original owner, a Loyalist, built it in 1796 on the Detroit side of the river. Not wanting the house to remain in American possession, he had the building dismantled, moved, and then reconstructed on this site. The numbering on the logs used to reassemble the house is still evident. The museum depicts life of the last century.

Amherstburg is one of Ontario's oldest towns with over a dozen buildings dating to before 1850. Most are situated in the Heritage District between the river and Sandwich Street (Highway 18). There's a walking tour brochure available at the Tourist Office (King's Navy Yard) or from local merchants. The age of this community is evident in the modest frame-style architecture which may be a surprise to visitors from other parts of the province. For comparison, see the homes near 450 Dalhousie, built in the more lavish Victorian style of the 1870s.

One of the most beautiful old buildings is the Salmoni Hotel at Dalhousie and Richmond, built of yellow and red brick in 1849. It is now the Navy Yard Bar and Grill, with a pleasant combination of history, river view and good food. The Navy Yard area marks the original British shipyard, which is now a lovely park. There are plans to complete construction of the HMS *Detroit*, a replica ship from the last century, and to have it docked at the yard.

Tourist shopping is located throughout town, but is concentrated in the Heritage District. Most browsable is Huntley's Emporium on Dalhousie Street. As if to reinforce the British claim to Amherstburg, Huntley's is filled to the rafters with British items, from gooseberries in syrup to tea towels decorated with collies. Just down the street at the Sandpiper Gallery is a huge collection of fine art, mainly wildlife, landscapes and historic scenes. It is well worth visiting.

There is one other place in town with historic connections, and it is a "must see" for daytrippers. The North American Black Historical Museum and Cultural Centre is on King Street, two blocks east of Sandwich. (En route visit the Gibson Gallery, with changing fine art exhibits, housed in a nineteenth-century train station.) Well-executed displays and films describe the history of Ontario's Blacks, focusing on Essex County. Most arrived here as fugitive slaves during the 1850s, although there were also United Empire Loyalists, British soldiers, and Canadian slaves emancipated in 1843. Maps, diagrams and letters tell the heart-rending story of the British slave trade, in which about 2.8 million Blacks were taken from Africa to the New World. Any visitor will find the history of the famous "Underground Railway" exciting. There are maps of routes and of the local towns that began as fugitive-slave settlements. There are even the words to a song slaves used to communicate information on the timing and direction of an escape. The museum also chronicles the contributions of Blacks to Ontario, as lawyers, educators, scientists and inventors.

Amherstburg is not only for history buffs. For those wanting more excitement, there is Boblo Island, a 90-year-old amusement park in the Detroit River. During the summer ferries leave every 15 minutes from a dock a couple of kilometres south of Amherstburg.

Boblo also has over 75 rides and continual entertainment. Boblo Island comprises over 120 hectares, with one-third used as parkland for picnicking, biking and lounging.

Amherstburg has a little something for everyone. Absorb a little history, have a meal and a stroll in pleasant surroundings, and enjoy a riverside drive on the way home.

Fort Malden
June 1-Labour Day:
Daily 10:00-6:00
Labour Day-May 31:
Daily 10:00-5:00
(519) 736-5416

Park House Museum
June-August:
Daily 9:00-5:00
September-May:
Tuesday-Friday 11:00-5:00
Sunday 11:00-5:00
(519) 736-2511

North American Black
Historical Museum
March-November:
Wednesday-Friday 10:00-5:00
Saturday & Sunday 1:00-5:00
(519) 736-5433

Amherstburg

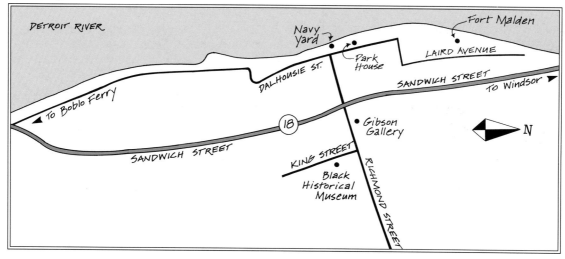

2 WINDSOR
Windsor Walkabout

Windsor is unique. What other city is located on native prairie, faces an international waterway, has an agreeable climate, and is small enough to tour in a single day? Because Windsor is an out-of-doors town, this is an overview of Windsor from the perspective of its special green places.

Jackson Park, at Ouelette and Tecumseh, is one of Windsor's most recommended sights. It has two exceptional gardens. Windsor's claim to the title "City of Roses" is unchallenged at the Rose Test Garden. Over 12,000 roses of 500 varieties are grown in beds arranged by colour and bush type. Windsor's long growing season means that there are roses in bloom from the beginning of June to October. The Sunken Garden has perennial beds brimming with colour, texture and fragrance.

Take either Ouelette Avenue or McDougall Street and head towards Detroit's fabulous skyline. (Natives will be sure to point out that you are travelling *north*.) Parking can be found near the Windsor Public Market at McDougall and Chatham. The market is indoors, but there's plenty of greenery here.

This may not be one of Ontario's biggest farm markets, but it is one of the best. The hours are convenient — all day, six days a week. Windsor is in the heart of Ontario's vegetable country, so the produce is fresh, fresh, fresh. And there is an excellent variety of vegetables, poultry, cheese, fresh fish and cut flowers. Best of all, there's Adler's Bakery, with more kinds of coffee cake than can be dreamed of. There are several diners in the market, each one living nostalgia, with vinyl-covered swivel stools, milkshakes in metal containers, and menus of ham n' eggs and grilled cheese.

Leave your car at the market or park near the river, and head for Dieppe Gardens at the end of Ouelette, the best place for taking in the gardens and the beautiful river views.

Windsor

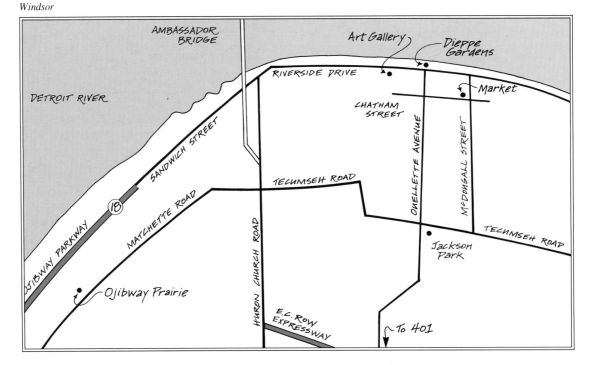

For about 200 years the Detroit River has been main street to both Detroit and Windsor, with ferries acting as streetcars, linking businesses and families. Today the Detroit River is the world's busiest waterway, and huge international tankers — "1,000-footers" — pass every half an hour or so. In addition to these behemoths, the river is filled with pleasure craft of every description, many flying along at breakneck speed.

A front-row view of Detroit is one of the nicest things about Windsor. The view features a photogenic combination of art deco skyscrapers and the glistening cylinders of the Renaissance Centre. Don't miss the breathtaking skyline at night. Better yet, visit during the July 1st to 4th Freedom Festival and watch fireworks over the river. An integral part of the river scene since 1929, the Ambassador Bridge was the answer to river-crossing problems that date to the 1700s.

Time for lunch or dinner. It is a safe bet that Windsor has more restaurants than any other city of similar size. And each restaurant specializes in food of a different ethnic origin. Wander the downtown for whatever appeals, from Italian to Cajun, bistro to pub. For those who can't take their eyes off the river, The Tugboat Restaurant is the only place in town. The Tugboat is permanently moored at the foot of Ouelette. It's a real Great Lakes tug, commissioned in 1911, with fore-to-aft woodwork and plenty of nautical paraphernelia. The river view is unequalled, and besides, there's no other restaurant where you can eat while being rocked by large swells. The menu features fresh fish, and both the food and the service deserve high ratings.

Windsor has several points of interest away from the river. For the art lover, the Art Gallery of Windsor is on Riverside Drive, a few blocks west of downtown. The extensive collection of Canadian paintings is arranged to illustrate the development of Canadian art over two centuries.

For the nature lover, Windsor's Ojibway Prairie Park is unique in Ontario. It is on Matchette Road; follow the map for your route. The Ojibway Prairie has several habitat types, but the big draw for naturalists from around the province is the tall-grass prairie. This is a tiny remnant of the lush green tapestry that once covered much of southwestern Ontario, Michigan and Ohio.

Across the street from the nature centre is a dead-end road (part of the Windsor bikeway system), and a short walk leads to an elevated lookout. There is also a trail right through the heart of the tall-grass. The prairie is not just grasses, but scores of wildflowers, such as black-eyed Susan, smooth aster, prairie loosestrife and grey-headed coneflower. Butterflies and birds flit around your ears. The displays at the nature centre do a good job of helping visitors identify interesting prairie flora and fauna. There are lots of hands-on and nature trivia games for children. The centre is open daily year-round.

Daytrippers will leave Windsor pleased and surprised that a large industrial city could offer so much green space for a day outdoors.

Art Gallery of Windsor
Tuesday, Wednesday &
Saturday 11:00-5:00
Thursday & Friday 11:00-9:00
Sunday 1:00-5:00
(519) 258-7111

3 WALKERVILLE
The Town that Walker Built

This trip tells about how a single individual, through energy and enterprise, met with success in business and influenced the fate of an entire community. Walkerville is now a part of northern Windsor, and today's trip explores the legacy of its founder, Hiram Walker.

The story begins at the best-known result of Hiram's activities, the Walker Distillery. The plant is impossible to miss, just navigate toward the grain elevators on Windsor's Riverside Drive. Public tours are given twice each weekday from June to September, except for a July shutdown period. Inquire at the reception office at Riverside and Walker Road (reservations essential).

The tour is one hour in length and covers every facet of the distilling operation. Grain, usually corn, rye or barley, is cooked and steam is forced through the fermenting mash; the alcohol is then distilled, and the liquid is stored in oak casks for about six years. It sounds simple enough, but it looks anything but simple when you take the plant tour and stand atop a five-storey fermentation tank. The entire plant is computerized and mechanized. Visitors watch casks being emptied and liquor bottled, sealed and labelled, all in a few moments without the touch of a human hand.

The plant tour also provides interesting details on Hiram Walker's rise from a humble grocer on the Michigan frontier. Hiram realized that there was more money in whisky than grain, so he began distilling. When distilling became illegal in Michigan in 1855, he moved across the Detroit River. In the last century, whisky was sold in unmarked casks, but Hiram's business sense led him to an innovative step: marketing his product in expensive glass bottles labelled with his name. This decision, like all his others, had the touch of success from its inception, and Walker's Distillery never looked back. Along the way, the Walker

family expanded into lumber, furniture and construction, to meet the demand for worker housing and municipal services in Walkerville. Today the Walker empire is known as Hiram Walker-Allied Vintners and has operations worldwide.

While at the plant don't miss admiring the original company offices, built in 1858 by Detroit architect Albert Kahn. (We'll be meeting him again later.) The charming building is soft buff-orange stone with a magnificent wrought-iron gate. Behind the offices lies a perfect little garden, a popular location for wedding photos.

Next visit is Willistead Manor, home of Hiram's son, E. Chandler Walker, and his wife, Mary Griffin Walker. Informative and good-humoured public tours are offered several days a week during the summer. The tours are a good way to find out about executive life away from the plant. Drive east on Walker to Niagara; Willistead is two blocks south.

Willistead, the gatehouse and coach house were all designed by Albert Kahn. Construction of the main home was from 1904 to 1906, and it is in the style of a British Tudor manor house. Looks are deceiving, since the building is actually reinforced concrete with a Tudor facade of half-timber, brick and stone. Walker occupied Willistead until his death in 1915; his wife continued to live here intermittently until 1921, when the home was deeded to the town. Willistead Manor is furnished according to the period, albeit sparsely.

It is clear that no expense was spared at Willistead. Austrian woodcarving genius Joachim Jungwrith created doors, panelling and mantelpieces that are massive in scale but delicate in detail. The home is filled with secret doors, many of which lead to outdoor patios. The most ingenious, however, leads from the entrance to the upper storey.

Hiram Walker-Allied Vintners offices

That way, the man of the house could avoid a gauntlet of female attention if he arrived home during his wife's social gatherings.

The division of family and social life along the lines of gender is obvious at Willistead. The billiard room is dark oak panelling and decorated with sporting pictures — decidedly masculine. The drawing room, according to the fashion of the day, is finished in silk damask. Although the carving is still present, it has been enamelled in pastel blue. We don't need the tiara holder to tell us who was in charge here.

After touring Willistead, take a breather in the six-hectare park, complete with playground, picnic tables and privy. It might be a good idea to bring a lunch with you, and to have it here at Willistead. The other choice for lunch is Chez Gyliane, serving Continental cuisine at 1880 Wyandotte Street East (closed Sunday). The first weekend in June marks Art-in-the-Park, a two-day art festival.

The neighbourhood surrounding Willistead is one of lovely homes of the well-to-do. To the east of the park, opposite the conservatory, is a grey home called Edgewood. Mrs. Walker had it built for her sister, but it was not enough to entice her sibling to move from Washington. While touring the neigh-bourhood, don't miss lovely St. Mary's Church, built by the Walker family for the townspeople. It is located across Niagara Street from Willistead and exhibits more wonderful work by carver Jungwrith.

Not only did Hiram Walker build one of this country's most successful enterprises, but he left a legacy of beautiful buildings and parks. Enjoy the day in the town that Walker built.

Hiram Walker-Allied Vintners (tours)
June-August:
Monday to Friday 10:00 and 2:00
Closed three weeks during July
Reservations essential
(519) 254-5171

Willistead Manor
September-June:
1st and 3rd Sunday each month
1:00-4:00
July & August:
Sunday-Wednesday 1:00-4:00
December:
Sunday 1:00-4:00
Wednesday 7-9PM
(519) 255-6534

4 HARROW
A Harrowing Experience

Today's trip is an eye-opener for those who think that farming is a matter of planting a seed, watching the sky, and taking the harvest to market. Success in agribusiness demands the meticulous study of crop pathology, weed science, pest control, irrigation, and greenhouse design, to name but a few topics. There's no better place in Ontario to survey the various forms of modern agriculture than in Essex County.

An agricultural tour must begin at the Harrow Agricultural Research Station. It is located on Highway 18 at the eastern end of town. Public tours are conducted weekdays year-round, with the winter tours indoors only and summer tours both in- and out-doors. But even if the official tour schedule doesn't fit with your plans, call ahead to arrange a private tour; the staff are pleased to oblige. Public tours begin with a 20-minute slide presentation, an overview of research station activities. A walking or wagon-ride tour of 30 to 40 minutes follows.

Over 40 hectares of the station are devoted to field trials, and these trials are the focus of the tour. There are plots of cereal crops testing soil fertility; of tree fruits testing disease and insect resistance; of tomatoes testing cold hardiness; of vegetables testing biological pest control and degradable pesticides.

The time-consuming process of testing crop varieties and methods of culture doesn't stop outside. Visitors also tour indoor laborator-ies where carefully controlled experiments are conducted concerning insect behaviour, greenhouse construction, optimum nutrient levels and tissue culture. One comes away with a respect for the scientists willing to repeat each meticulous step of an experiment as many times as is necessary to reach reliable conclusions.

With greater appreciation for the science of modern farming, it is time to see some of the results. Drive east on Highway 18 from Harrow to Kingsville. It's one roadside market after another, offering everything from apples to zucchini; some are ready-picked, some are pick-your-own. Stock up for a picnic and for the home freezer.

This is a landscape different from any other in Ontario. Beyond the farmhouses, and in rows from Harrow to Leamington, there are greenhouses as far as the eye can see. It seems that every available scrap of soil is under glass. The first time these vegetables see the out-of-doors is on the market table; perhaps that is why they are so blemish-free.

Although southwestern Ontario is known as vegetable and fruit-tree country, grape-growing is becoming more popular. The conditions in Essex County, with nitrogen-rich soil and a temperate climate, are perfect for demanding vine crops. And the results of patience in establishing a grower network and marketing skills are paying off for a number of young Essex wineries, as they make names for themselves in wine competi-tions. Several of the wineries have public tours offering an insider's view of wine-making.

The hours and convenient location of the Pelee Island Winery make it a winner for this daytrip. It is located on Highway 18 on the east side of Kingsville. Tours begin with a 20-minute slide presentation. Visitors then tour the plant, beginning with the fermentation casks and ending with the bottling plant. A wine-tasting follows; non-alcoholic beverages are also available. There is a store on the premises.

Pelee Island Winery was established in 1980, harvesting the first crop in 1983. Although one of the newest wineries, Pelee Island is growing fast and has a capacity of about 70,000 cases. Grapes are harvested from nearby Pelee Island and processed within hours in Kingsville.

Grape press, Pelee Island Winery

Colasanti's has a large gift shop with good prices on pots, fertilizer and plants. They also make things easy for daytrippers by providing a full-service cafeteria. Arrive early in the day, when the muffins and cookies are hot from the oven.

From tomatoes to grapes to palm trees, Essex County grows it all for you.

Pelee Island was chosen as the best region for grape-farming because the growing season is actually longer than that of the traditional wine-making regions of Europe. The season is so long that this winery is one of few able to produce the coveted "ice wines," made from grapes that grow until the hard frosts of December. The result is a rare wine, made even rarer by the price — about one hundred dollars a litre.

Colio Wines in Harrow also provides public tours with tastings. They are located on Walker Road in Harrow (turn north off Highway 3 on to Walker, in the middle of town).

It's probably time to find a place to eat. Either picnic at the beach in Kingsville (follow Division Street south to the lake) or eat at one of the many good restaurants in town.

And now for something completely different. Continue east on Highway 18 to County Road 45; follow signs at Concession 3 for Colasanti's Tropical Gardens. Under one-and-a-half hectares of glass, the Colasanti family grows just about everything going. There are masses of indoor foliage plants, cacti of every shape and size, and flowering plants from orchids to lilies. And for children, there's a petting zoo with goats, ponies, and even a llama. It's a toss-up as to whether the caged tropical birds or the flowers are more brilliantly coloured, but the birds are much noisier.

Harrow Agricultural
Research Station (tours)
November-April:
Monday-Friday 8:15-4:30
July-October:
Tuesday & Thursday 2:00
(519) 738-2251

Pelee Island Winery (tours)
April-December:
Monday-Saturday 12:00, 2:00 and 4:00
December-March:
Saturday 12:00, 2:00 and 4:00
(retail store)
Monday-Friday 9:00-5:00
Saturday 10:00-5:00
(519) 733-6551

Colio Wines (tours)
Wednesday 1:00
Saturday 12:00-4:00
(retail store)
Monday-Saturday 9:00-5:00
(519) 726-5317

Colasanti's Tropical Gardens
Monday-Thursday 8:00-5:00
Friday-Sunday 8:00-7:00
(519) 326-3287

5 KINGSVILLE
Local Hero

Kingsville is a good daytrip destination for many reasons: beaches, shopping, dining, bird-watching. But Kingsville is best known as the home of the Jack Miner Sanctuary for wild waterfowl. The sanctuary attracts visitors who want to see the birds as well as pay tribute to one of the fathers of modern nature conservation. From Kingsville, drive north on Division Street to Concession 3, and be on the lookout for the signs at the corner.

The best times to see Canada geese in the tens of thousands are in late March and late November. Each day during October and November, at 3 and 4 PM, the birds are flushed into flight. This is one of Ontario's most impressive shows of motion and sound. But a visit during the rest of the year is also rewarding, since there are many species of

Miner Statue, Kingsville

birds permanently resident here. And there is always a bucket of grain for feeding them — a hit with the kids.

The Jack Miner Museum chronicles Miner's achievements as a conservationist and public figure, making use of the wide coverage his career received in newspaper articles and photographs. Miner's proficiency as a hunt-guide in turn-of-the-century Essex won him a wide reputation among prominent people of the day, such as Thomas Edison and Henry Ford. Concerned with the overhunting of waterfowl, Miner began attracting wild Canada geese to his brickyard pond. The program was so successful that the migration patterns of huge numbers of geese were permanently altered, a result completely unexpected by ornithologists of the time.

Thus Miner embarked on a career that produced three books (from a man lacking formal education) and lecture tours from Alaska to the Waldorf Astoria. Our hero also started a bird-banding program (another first). A Bible verse was stamped on each band, so that Miner became a long-distance missionary to the hunters of the Hudson Bay Lowlands, where the geese summered. Jack Miner was instrumental in the designation of Point Pelee as a national park, in ending the practice of lure-hunting, and in the passage of the International Migratory Bird Act.

King George VI bestowed Miner with the O.B.E.; encyclopedias of the day consistently listed Miner as among the world's 15 or 20 greatest people; and the week of his birth (April 10) is National Wildlife Week in Canada. From diplomats to tycoons, famous people from around the world have visited the sanctuary. This is the only place where one can stand on the same ground as Sir Wilfrid Laurier, Ty Cobb, Henry Ford, Norman Vincent Peale, Stanley Kresge and Mackenzie King. They came as admirers and left as good friends. Their visits are recorded in letters, photographs and personal momentoes.

The remainder of the day can be spent in Kingsville. Kingsville offers so many different things to do, it would be a worthwhile daytrip even without its close proximity to Jack Miner's.

For a small town, Kingsville has a good variety of eating places. Four spots deserve special mention. Best for lunch is The Rose and Thistle Tea Room (64 Main East). The fare is definitely British, and there are even two different afternoon teas offered: English and Scots (hence the name). An abundance of fresh local fruit and berries means lots of luscious desserts for summer visitors. Fine continental dining is alive and well at The Vintage Goose (12 Pearl Street, one street south of Main). No Erie town is complete without a fish restaurant, and Kingsville has two: the Lakeshore Terrace Hotel and King's Landing, next door to each other on Park Street near the lake.

Shoppers will have some browsing to do in Kingsville. Pelee Wings is a welcome perch for birders, offering a full selection of birding and bird-feeding accessories: binoculars, feeders, games, records, tapes, prints, tapestries. Pelee Wings is also a pretty bed-and-breakfast with "early-bird" breakfasts. Fireside Antiques at 25 Division Street North has an excellent range of lamps and clocks. Division Street has several arts and crafts stores spread out from downtown to the lake. The largest, Kingfisher's Studio, is at Number 20.

By the time you've reached the lake, you'll be ready for one of the benches at Lakeside Park, and the kids will be ready for the large playground and beach.

One other attraction near town is worth mentioning. The John R. Park Homestead is located on County Road 50 west of Kingsville; the easiest route is to follow the lakeshore west to the Park Conservation Area. The home is an oddity in rural Ontario, a frame Greek Revival farmhouse built in the 1830s. That it has any architectural theme at all is a tribute to the wealth of merchant, shipper, farmer and lumberman John R. Park. The restored homestead reflects life in the mid-1800s. There are plenty of year-round special events and activities on the farm for young and old alike. But most captivating of all is the site — you can practically dabble your toes in Lake Erie while standing on the back porch.

Whether you visit Kingsville for the wild geese and stay for its quiet ambience, or the other way around, you'll be educated and entertained by a visit to Canada's southernmost town.

Jack Miner Sanctuary
Daily, year-round:
9:00-5:00
Closed Sunday
(519) 733-4034

John R. Park Homestead
mid-May to end-June & September:
Monday-Friday 10:00-4:00
Sunday 12:00-4:00
July-Labour Day:
Daily 10:00-4:00
October to mid-May:
Monday-Friday 10:00-4:00
(519) 738-2029

6 LEAMINGTON
Spitting Image

The name Pelee sends a shiver of excitement through every Ontario bird-watcher. Point Pelee National Park, Canada's southern tip, is rated as one of North America's birding hot spots. And yet, as any visitor quickly learns, this slender V of sand jutting out into Lake Erie is not only for the birds, since there is surely something here for everyone.

Pelee owes its reputation for bird-watching to the fact that it is where two major bird migration routes converge. It is also the shortest distance across the hazardous open water of Lake Erie. Consequently, spring (March to May) and fall (September to November) are the most productive seasons for bird-watchers. The trees drip with warblers and the air is filled with a cacophony of calls; farmer's fields are speckled with gulls and shorebirds; and large rafts of ducks mass in Lake Erie. Whether an expert, a novice, or a bemused bystander, you are sure to be impressed by the number and diversity of birds at Pelee in any season.

Monarch butterflies also use Point Pelee as the easiest route across Lake Erie. During heavy migrations, usually in late September, the shrubs near the Tip are covered with a fluttering orange blanket.

Pelee's greatest reward to the naturalist is its remarkable diversity — there's so many different types of habitat in such a limited space. This makes it easy to study plants and animals from a wide geographic range without actually travelling very far. It's possible to see a prickly pear cactus (from the southwestern States), a hop-tree (from the southeastern States), and a swamp rose-mallow (limited to a few Lake Erie marshes), all in the space of a few hours, not to mention dunes and beaches, dry and wet woodlands, and marsh, all with their characteristic flora and fauna.

The best place to begin exploring Pelee is at the Park Visitor Centre. Movies, displays and trail pamphlets, along with friendly, expert staff, will brief you on what you should keep your eyes and ears ready for. Park naturalists also prepare taped telephone messages during spring and fall to let prospective visitors know the progress of bird and butterfly movements.

There are five walking trails and one cycling trail at Pelee. Several are accessible to wheelchairs and strollers; ask at the interpretive centre for guidance. Bicycle and canoe rentals are at the concession near the marsh boardwalk. Washrooms are at the boardwalk, at the Tip, and at the interpretive centre.

The following capsule description of the walking trails may help you plan your day. (The cycling trail follows the main roadway.)

Tilden's Woods: a one-kilometre trail passes through lush, serene woodland that is reminiscent of the viny forests of the southern U.S. Tilden's is a good spot to look for elusive Connecticut, mourning and prothonotory warblers.

The Tip: a short trail leads from a concession stand to the end of the spit, the arrival and departure point for migrants. To see hundreds of people, bristling with cameras and binoculars, stand in the drizzle here at 5 AM is reminiscent of scenes from *Close Encounters of the Third Kind*.

Marsh Boardwalk: although this is not a particularly active place for nature-watchers, it has to be mentioned because the marsh covers two-thirds of Pelee's area, and because this must be one of the most photographed natural areas in Canada. A one-and-a-half-kilometre boardwalk snakes through a sea of cattails. Look for Blanding's and painted turtles, and marsh wrens.

Woodland Trail: many naturalists think that this three-kilometre walk which begins at the Visitor Centre is the best in the park. A

Marsh Boardwalk, Point Pelee

Walking the trails at Pelee, checklist and bird guide in hand, works up an appetite. The beach cuisine is not recommended, so unless you brought a picnic basket, you'll be heading out of the park.

There are numerous places to eat in Leamington, and several of these are worth noting. 13 Russell Street is the name and address of a restaurant with a fine reputation for local fish served in a historic home. The Tropicana, 311 Erie Street South, on Leamington's north-south drag, serves the best panzerotti in Ontario. The Dock Restaurant on the town wharf specializes in seafood and a great view.

Whether it is the birds, butterflies, plants, reptiles, amphibians, beaches or fishing that bring you here, you will leave with a greater appreciation of Point Pelee as one of the most intriguing natural areas in Ontario.

brochure points out highlights of three portions of this trail — wooded swamp, dry woodland and abandoned orchard. Look for fox snakes and white-tailed deer.

DeLaurier Trail: a testament to early settlement in Pelee, this trail starts at a restored farmhouse and leads to abandoned canals. Pelee's least-crowded trail, and the only one with its own parking lot, the DeLaurier Trail can be a good place to study field-dwelling species such as sparrows.

Pelee offers the daytripper a multitude of activities other than nature study. The park is open 24 hours a day when the smelt run in April; fisherfolk stay on the beach all night to catch and eat their fill of these silvery creatures. Several beaches are patrolled for swimming. Weather co-operating, there is skating and cross-country skiing in winter. Camping is limited to groups only; Wheatley Provincial Park is the nearest good camping.

Point Pelee National Park
Daily, year-round
(519) 326-3204

7 BLENHEIM
Birdland

Before European exploration and settlement, the fertile plain of southwestern Ontario supported forests of immense oak and pine, vast marshes, and in the extreme southwest, tall-grass prairie. In a scant century or so market gardening and cash crops have replaced the native vegetation, making the remaining natural areas precious, and none more so than Rondeau Provincial Park, that long spit of sand sticking out into Lake Erie between Blenheim and Ridgetown. Rondeau is reached via Highway 3.

Naturalists of all persuasions rate Rondeau as tops in the province. The park's 4,800 hectares probably support more different habitat types than most entire countries! There is dune, marsh, prairie, and dry oak and pine forests, for starters. But the star of the show is the Carolinian forest, the largest remaining area of these southern species in Ontario. This vegetation community contributes most of Rondeau's 600 plant species, including tuliptree and sassafras. Many of the park's 19 species of orchid are in its southern forests. The forest is so lush that it seems semi-tropical.

Rondeau is probably the best place to birdwatch in the entire province: 80 percent of the bird species found in Ontario can be seen in Rondeau, including 144 species that nest here. The most sought-out are the bald eagles, which nest in tall trees overlooking the bay marshes. Another favourite is the prothonotory warbler, attracted by Rondeau's Carolinian forests.

Rare reptiles and amphibians also make Rondeau their home, as most other suitable habitat in southern Ontario is being destroyed. In the marsh, look for the spiny soft-shell turtle and fox snakes, while near the beaches look for hog-nosed snakes and Fowler's toads.

There are so many ways to partake of Rondeau's unique habitats. There are five hiking trails, from 1 to 15 kilometres in length. Visitors are delighted by Rondeau's tranquility; even though located within a highly urbanized region, the park's trails are often deserted. White-tailed deer are often spotted while hiking the trails. Rondeau's flat topography and low traffic levels make

Rondeau Bay

it one of Ontario's preferred biking areas, and bike rentals are available just outside the park entrance.

Water activities abound at Rondeau. Swimmers can chose from 12 kilometres of Lake Erie beach and smaller beach areas on the warmer bay side of the peninsula. Rondeau is much beloved by canoeists, who can paddle along marsh channels to spot some of Ontario's rarer birds, reptiles and amphibians. Marinas near the park entrance rent canoes, boats and launching facilities. Bayside Boardsailing near the park entrance provides equipment and lessons for sailors and windsurfers. Lake Erie is rated the best pickerel fishery in Ontario, and there's also bass, perch and pike. Ice-fishing for perch is popular on Rondeau Bay.

Find out about a diversity of nature programs at the Visitor Centre. Special aspects of Rondeau's environment are highlighted during evening presentations at the centre. Naturalists also run group hikes, campfire programs, skits, contests and a children's program.

For lunch, one of the best bets of the day is to picnic in the park itself. There are a number of stores and small restaurants in the park. Alternatively, try A & L Country Market & Restaurant at the corner of Highways 3 and 51, just north of Rondeau. The specialties are fresh-caught fish and homemade baked goods, preserves and natural cheeses. Don't miss the vegetable stand, which offers a delectable array of local vegetables and fruits.

Mother Nature arranged geography, geology, botany and zoology to make Rondeau a truly special place. But special places can be developed through human activity as well. One example, the Greenview Aviaries and Game Farm, is located on Highway 3, one kilometre east of Morpeth.

Just six years in operation, Greenview's 100 or so species make it one of Ontario's largest private zoos. It is certainly one of the cleanest, most spacious and best organized. A thorough brochure is given to visitors, who are free to wander at will through the outdoor displays, as well as through the many buildings. Some of Greenview's more unusual animals are coatimudi, mutjac deer, ferrets, and a cavy. Visitors will be captivated by several species of monkey, all actively swinging, climbing and noisily chatting. There are also a host of domestic animals, from clownish goats to prize guinea pigs and cats.

But the stars of the show are the birds, from huge rheas to diminutive African finches. Ponds are filled with native and exotic geese, ducks and swans. Outdoor runs house more kinds of pheasant than you thought possible. Spacious indoor displays feature brilliant macaws, toucans and cockatoos, not to mention Amazonian parrots and a variety of chickens and turkeys.

Greenview makes every effort to be hospitable to children. There's a huge playground and sandbox, complete with construction toys. There are also coin-operated machines supplying grain for feeding the animals, an observation tower, baby-changing facilities and a miniature village.

From the diversity of Rondeau to a well-run private zoo, the Blenheim area has lots to offer the daytripper seeking southwestern Ontario's special places.

Greenview Aviaries and Game Farm
May-October:
Daily 9:00-8:00
(519) 674-3025

Rondeau Provincial Park
Daily, year-round
(519) 674-5405

8 CHATHAM
Follow the North Star

Uncle Tom's Cabin is a title familiar enough to most Ontarians, and we know that the novel recounts the efforts of American slaves to gain freedom in Canada, but few of us appreciate that this is a real story about real people, and that the story is an integral part of the development of southwestern Ontario.

At first glance the village of Dresden, northeast of Chatham, seems an ordinary rural town, but Dresden receives visitors from around the world on pilgrimages to Uncle Tom's Cabin Museum. The museum comprises a visitor centre and six buildings, which work together to tell the story of Josiah Henson, whose experiences as a slave and fugitive form the basis for much of Harriet Beecher Stowe's character Uncle Tom.

Henson was born into slavery in 1789. A capable man, he worked as an overseer and lay preacher. He purchased his freedom, only to lose it through deceit, and finally, in 1830, the Henson family "followed the North Star" and escaped to Ontario. Henson did not rest content with winning his own freedom. He co-founded the British American Institute and made lecture tours to raise funds. The Institute purchased 200 acres near Dresden (including the land the museum sits on) as the start of a mill community for escaped slaves.

Exhibits, brochures and taped commentary in the visitor centre provide details of slavery and Henson's life. There are authentic handcuffs, clubs and whips. Most visitors are surprised to find remnants of the Canadian slave trade, such as posters advertising slave auctions in York (Toronto). There are also exhibits relating to Stowe's enduring epic, first published in 1852. It sold over 300,000 copies that year alone and was translated into 27 languages.

Outside the visitor centre is Uncle Tom's Cabin, the weathered frame house that was Henson's home until his death in 1883. The furnishings, some of which are Henson's own, illustrate the humble existence typical of fugitive slaves. Next to Henson's home is the church he preached in, complete with original pulpit and organ. As with the cabin, note the handmade nails, evidence that fugitives had to meet all their own needs from very limited resources. To the front of the museum is the Henson family burial plot.

After visiting Uncle Tom's Cabin, drive south to Chatham via County Road 29 and Highway 40. During the last century, Chatham had the largest Black population of any Ontario town — perhaps as large as one-third of the town's population, and a vibrant Black community remains in Chatham today.

A church is at the heart of every Black settlement. Ontario's most famous Black church is Chatham's First Baptist Church at 135 King Street East, in the heart of Black Chatham. (Continue on Highway 40, cross the Thames River; the first left is King Street.) First Baptist is known as John Brown's Church, for it was here that the American plotted the famous raid on Harper's Ferry. A historical plaque stands on the church's front lawn.

Chatham is perhaps the prettiest town in southwestern Ontario, all shady streets and Victorian mansions. Tecumseh Park is in the centre of town both geographically and socially. There's always something going on here, from band concerts to lawn bowling. It is an ideal spot for a picnic, or for boat-watching along the river.

The early wealth of Chatham led to many fine homes being constructed, and a pleasant stroll can be had in any of the older neighbourhoods. One of the nicest is just west of downtown, location of the picturesque Kent Club. For restaurants, locals often recommend Cravings on Fifth Street near its

FOLLOW THE DRINKIN' GOURD

Slaves planning an escape to freedom on the Underground Railway needed to pass information in the presence of white masters. Cryptic messages were often hidden in the words of songs. In this particular song, the drinking gourd is the Big Dipper, the conductor is a man with a wooden leg and the river is the Ohio River.

When the sun comes back and the first quail calls,
Follow the drinking gourd.
For the old man is a-waitin' for to carry you to freedom,
If you follow the drinkin' gourd.

The riverbank will make a very good road.
The dead trees show you the way.
Left foot, peg foot, traveling on,
Following the drinkin' gourd.

(From the North American Black Historical Museum and Cultural Centre)

junction with King. Cravings specializes in light meals, take-out picnics, and luscious desserts (closed Sundays).

The settlement started by Henson was one of dozens of Black settlements in southwestern Ontario. Some have been incorporated with neighbouring towns, as Henson's was by Dresden; some disappeared, as fugitives returned to the United States following emancipation; and some communities exist intact. The best example of a Black community surviving from the days of fugitive slaves is North Buxton.

Drive south on Queen Street (County Road 10) and head west just after crossing the 401. Road 14 takes you to North Buxton. Buxton, originally the Elgin Settlement, was well known as a stop on the Underground Railway. The town started through the efforts of Irish-born Presbyterian minister, William King. King ensured that Buxton would become Canada's premier Black community by establishing a self-sufficient agricultural economy, a first-rate school (it became so popular with local Whites that the government school closed) and church.

The modest Raleigh Museum and its knowledgeable staff are dedicated to keeping alive the achievements of Buxton founders and residents. The work of local writers and artists is displayed, and there are some of King's personal belongings, the most interesting being his journal. A slide show details the history of Buxton.

Today's trip has followed the footsteps of tens of thousands of Blacks who came to Ontario as fugitive slaves. It will surprise many travellers to discover that Black heritage is an important part of Ontario's heritage.

Uncle Tom's Cabin Museum
mid-May to October:
Daily 10:00-5:00
(519) 683-2978

Raleigh Township Centennial Museum
May-September:
Wednesday-Sunday 1:00-4:30
Other times by appointment
(519) 352-4799

9 SARNIA
Life on the River

Summer on the St. Clair River

If the shores of the St. Clair River could talk, what tales they would tell! Sailors and shipwrecks; ore and oil; fish and fortunes. A green ribbon of shoreline from Wallaceburg to Sarnia is preserved as the St. Clair Parkway, a beauty spot for fishermen and boaters, a joy for the recreational driver, and breathing space for a river and its wildlife. Today's trip takes advantage of the foresight that provided the Parkway, as we sample a little of life on the river.

One of the highlights of the tour is a river cruise aboard the *Duc D'Orleans*, departing from Sarnia. Be wise and reserve a spot on the cruise, and then plan the rest of the day around that time; it will dictate whether the journey is north to south or vice versa. The driving tour described here begins at Sombra and ends at Sarnia.

Sombra, once a sleepy terminal for the car-ferry to Marine City, Michigan, has begun sprucing up for the tourist trade. For shoppers, there is a mock English village, with shops featuring a variety of vacation wear, crafts, fine art and tasty frozen treats. Near

the ferry dock is the Olde Ferry Inn, reputed to have been visited by Al Capone. It is currently under renovation. In an original pioneer home, the Sombra Township Museum has a few items related to shipping on the river, such as a sextant, sailor's palm, and a piece of LaSalle's ship, the *Griffon*. There's a large collection of historical photos of lake freighters and cruise ships.

From Sombra to Sarnia, the Parkway is one riverside park after another, and each is terrific for admiring the St. Clair. The star of the day is the water itself: indescribably vivid, mesmerizingly turquoise. If you saw this colour in a photograph, you would say that it had been retouched. The only other way to see water this colour is on an Aegean cruise; save yourself a few thousand dollars and stop awhile on the Parkway.

The St. Clair River is good fishing water, and there are plenty of breakwalls for superintending a bobber. Boat-launching ramps are located in several parks. Sailboats, freighters, yachts, tugs — boat-watchers can spend a day in heaven. Several of the parks

26

have sandy beaches, and all have picnic spots. Two of the largest parks, Cathcart and Lambton-Cundick, are just north of Sombra and have camping facilities.

The Moore Museum is the next stop. Of interest to the Parkway traveller is the Marine room. Navigational equipment, models, a lake captain's logbook, and cruise ship memorabilia (yes, the Great Lakes used to be active with large cruise ships!) illustrate life on the Great Lakes. Most captivating of all are the exhibits describing the toll of ships and lives taken by the Great Lakes. There is a map with locations of shipwrecks on the St. Clair River, and detailed descriptions of how they sank, whether by storm, explosion or collision; some are simply reported as lost at sea.

There is a championship public golf course at Mooretown, run by the Parkway Commission, as well as indoor and outdoor swimming, and camping.

Continue north on the Parkway, through the awesome landscape of petrochemical plants at Corunna. Locals and tourists alike visit Corunna after dark to see millions of lights sparkle on the cracking towers and storage tanks. Oil refining began in this area in 1862, and a list of companies attracted by the oil resources and the convenient location sounds like a who's-who of industry: Dow Chemical, Polysar, Esso, Du Pont, Allied Chemical, C.I.L., Dome Petroleum, Monsanto, Petrosar, Union Carbide, Shell.

Each of these giant firms has a story to tell. At Dow, salt is brought to the surface from 600 metres below and used to produce caustic chemicals. Polysar, the area's largest single employer, produces rubber and plastic. Esso, the largest petrochemical plant in Sarnia, refines 130,000 barrels of oil daily, and the plant runs 365 days a year, 24 hours a day. Note the Shell fueling dock; it is the largest on the Great Lakes.

Proceed through Sarnia to the waterfront (follow Highway 40B signs to Wellington, turn west to Front Street). The *Duc d'Orleans* is docked at Mackenzie Park. It is a renovated World War II sub-chaser, built in Sarnia in 1944. The *Duc* takes up to 200 passengers at a time for sightseeing, lunch and dinner cruises; the cruises take two or three hours. Passengers have a choice view of the mansions on the American side of the river from Port Huron to Marysville. The cruise passes near lake freighters; commentary from the wheelhouse provides details of cargo, size, ownership and history. The river is crammed with pleasure craft on summer weekends and it is quite entertaining to watch them narrowly avoid collision.

There's more in store for the tourist upon disembarking back at Sarnia. There are ambitious plans for the waterfront. The first stage of a master plan for the Sarnia Marina is in place, with spaces for hundreds of boats. The Marina Restaurant has a good view but is usually open only until mid-afternoon. Canatara Park on Lake Huron (at the north end of Christina Street) has 1,000 metres of white sandy beach. This is a prime boat-watching post, since navigation-wise you are sitting at the wide end of a funnel. Canatara also has a children's zoo, sports fields and historic buildings. During the winter there is skiing and skating.

You will head home very glad indeed that the St. Clair Parkway Commission has saved this precious edge of the river, allowing us to rest our eyes on the bluest of blue waters.

Duc D'Orleans Cruise
June to September: Sunday 10:30, 2:30
Monday-Saturday 12:00
(519) 337-5152

Moore Museum
March-November:
Wednesday-Sunday 10:00-5:00
(519) 867-2020

Sombra Museum
May & September:
Saturday & Sunday 2:00-5:00
June-August: Daily 2:00-5:00
(519) 892-3631

10 PETROLIA
Petrol Power

Oil Springs? Oil City? Petrolia? This must be Alberta — or Texas. The names certainly don't sound Ontarian, but there they are, southeast of Sarnia, on the wide prairie of southwestern Ontario. There is usually an interesting story behind the naming of settlements, and the stories behind these three are no exception. This daytrip explores Petrolia and vicinity — gushers, oil boom-towns and industrial revolution.

Petrolia is located west of Highway 21, 13 kilometres south of Highway 402. The first visit of the day is to Petrolia Discovery, just east of town, across from the Bridgeview Conservation Area.

This is a working museum. Most of Petrolia Discovery's 25 hectares are an authentic oil field, with 14 wells producing a tiny but steady flow of 225 barrels a month. The fascination at Petrolia is that these wells are still being worked as they have been for over 100 years. In fact, the ceaseless creaking and groaning of the jerker lines is likely to be the visitor's most vivid and lasting impression of Petrolia.

Start by viewing the NFB film *Hard Oil*. Next come photographic pavilions with a fine collection describing the nineteenth-century oil industry, the corporate evolution of Imperial Oil (our own indigenous petroleum giant), and modern oil exploration and refining. The best part of a visit to Petrolia Discovery is the tour of the oil field. There is a guiding brochure, or better yet, take a personal tour led by the knowledgeable staff.

The oil field displays are a history of an industry in its infancy. Oilmen were drawn to Petrolia for the asphalt in local "gum-beds." But it wasn't until James Miller Williams developed a method for refining kerosene (the first advance in lighting in 8,000 years) that Petrolia became an oil town. At one time, there were about 10,000 wells in the Petrolia fields alone! The boom lasted from about 1860 to the turn of the century, although there are still hundreds of active wells in the area.

There are displays of early digging and drilling equipment. Because southern Ontario was the centre of the early oil industry, methods and tools developed in Petrolia — rigs, tank trucks, pumping stations, pipelines, refining stills and towers — became the standard of practice around the world. Methods and machinery invented here won scientific acclaim, and fabulous wealth, for locals such as John Henry Fairbanks (the jerker line system) and Frederick Fitzgerald (the Fitzgerald rig or pumping station; he was to become Imperial's first president).

Petrolia Discovery will fuel your curiosity for more oil touring. Head into town. Not a great deal has changed since the oil bust at the turn of the century. The oil industry still dominates the town: even the streetlight standards are miniature oil rigs. The Victorian Opera House, hospital and train station all survive. Summer theatre is performed in the Opera House (under repair for recent fire damage); the train station is now the public library. An interesting lunch spot is the Oil Rig Restaurant, just south of the main street, on Centre Street. The rustic decor includes pictures of old Petrolia and the portraits of local oil heroes. The Fairbanks home at the east end of town on Petrolia Street is now an antique shop.

The second museum stop of the day is in Oil Springs, where James Williams drilled the first commercial oil well in North America. It is on the property of the Oil Museum of Canada. From Petrolia, drive east to Highway 21, and south 11 kilometres to Oil Springs; road signs direct you to the museum on a large property near the southeast corner of town.

The introductory displays in the museum review the importance of oil to modern society: heating and transportation, synthetic fabrics, machine lubrication, solvents, and cosmetics are all petroleum dependent or derived. There is also information about petroleum geology, extraction and refining. An honour roll lists the hundreds of local residents who took Canadian oil know-how across the globe to oil fields in over 67 countries, from Indonesia to Venezuela.

ROCK GLEN

There is an interesting side trip to the Petrolia oil tour. The Rock Glen Conservation Area near Arkona is the ideal place to study petroleum geology first-hand. The strong erosive action of the Rock Glen and Ausable rivers has carved steep gorges, and in the process, washed out fossils from layers of rock previously hidden deep below the surface. About 400 million years ago, this area was covered by a sea teeming with plants and animals. The sea bed was formed into sedimentary rock, and the remains of plants and animals compressed into fossils, or into oil deposits, depending on geologic conditions.

The sharp-eyed fossil hunter, whether veteran or novice, can spend a few minutes or a few hours in the park, hunting for brachiopods, trilobites, corals and other species. The Conservation Authority permits each seeker to collect one specimen of each variety found and confines the searching (no digging, please!) to specific areas.

Open to visitors year-round, the park is also good for hiking, fishing, cross-country skiing, snowshoeing and picnicking.

Perhaps the most fascinating part of the museum is the history of Oil Springs itself — the quintessential boomtown. After Williams struck oil here, Oil Springs blossomed overnight from a crossroads town to a settlement of 4,000. Half a dozen years later, however, the oilmen had moved to Petrolia, and Oil Springs was left as a ghost town of 300. As a quaint reminder, the Morningstar Oil Producers on Main Street sells oil industry antiques, such as machinery, tools, kerosene lamps and oil gauges.

The Oil Museum of Canada has produced an interesting driving-tour brochure. The tour points out examples of the technology seen at Petrolia Discovery, much of it still in current production, such as the jerker lines still creaking away on the Fairbanks' farm.

As you make for home in your petroleum-fueled car, remember that it was the ingenuity and resourcefulness of the folks of Petrolia that made it all possible. In the process, Lambton became the world's first OPEC — Oil Producing and Exporting County.

Petrolia Discovery
May-Labour Day:
Daily 10:00-6:00
September & October:
Monday-Friday 9:00-5:00
(519) 882-0095

Oil Museum of Canada
May-October:
Daily 10:00-5:00
November-April:
Monday-Friday 10:00-12:00 and
1:00-5:00
(519) 834-2840

Oil Rig Restaurant
Daily, year-round 11:00-10:00
(519) 882-1232

11 GRAND BEND
The Alternative Grand Bend

During the winter, Grand Bend peacefully caters to skiers. But in the summer, the village swells to 50,000 persons, most of whom are walking or driving along the main street. For city-dwellers, Grand Bend is definitely not the place to get away from it all. But take heart: there is an alternative Grand Bend that lets us have our sandy dunes and holiday atmosphere without the hassle. It's all in the knowing how.

A day on the breezy Huron shores must start at Pinery Provincial Park. It lies just south of Grand Bend proper, although it seems a million kilometres away from the pandemonium. The Pinery once had a reputation for noisy crowds, but the Ministry of Natural Resources has been successful in returning the park to the people who want to enjoy its extraordinary natural beauty.

The Pinery has over 2,500 hectares of pine-oak forest, meadow and marsh. But most people visit for the beach: 10 kilometres of fine sand and magnificent dunes. It's a perfect setting for picnics. The Old Ausable Channel runs through the park, behind the foredunes. It was initially dug to drain farmland, but is now fed by springs underneath the dunes. The water is clear, unpolluted, and supports a diversity of fish, ducks, insects, beaver and deer. The channel is a tranquil place to fish and canoe. Pinery has over 80 kilometres of interior roads, which can be best enjoyed by bicycle (bikes and canoes can be rented at the park concession). Most visitors will want to spend the better part of a day on the beach, which is wonderfully uncrowded, even on summer long weekends.

Pinery Provincial Park is beloved by naturalists. The list of notable wildlife and plants seems to go on and on. A few of the rarer residents include the Olympus butterfly, five-lined skink, eastern bluebird, prairie warbler, and the hog-nosed snake. Nine trails, varying in length from one to three kilometres, teach hikers about dune ecology, marshland, and forest management. The Riverside Trail is wheelchair accessible. All of these walks offer a good chance to see white-tailed deer, and most have terrific lookouts.

Visitors will be especially interested in learning about the use of deliberately set fires to maintain the open oak forest and meadow at the Pinery. This strategy was used by Indians to reduce the growth of trees and maintain meadow habitat for deer and grouse. Prairie plants and herbs thrive in such forest openings. The goal is to provide conditions suitable for the graceful wild lupine, and the Karner blue butterfly which depends on the flower.

Park naturalists conduct walking tours, organize skits and slide presentations, run

Pinery Provincial Park

children's nature programs, and do anything else necessary to help visitors appreciate the unique amalgamation of beach, forest, bog and dune that they call the Pinery. You'll likely be so captivated by all the Pinery has to offer the naturalist that you will want to stay longer; don't worry, there are over 1,000 campsites here, most available by reservation.

Winter visitors will be happy to learn that there are 42 kilometres of rolling trails for skiing and hiking, tobogganing, and a skating rink, with warming hut and fire. (In fact, for a real alternative Grand Bend, come in the winter, when the park takes on a special silvery beauty.)

After an introduction to the natural processes which continue to form the fragile landscape along Lake Huron, it's time to find out how people fit into the picture. Just north of the park, and on the other side of Highway 21, is the Lambton Heritage Museum. This is a real winner among local museums. The museum brings the early settlers, their hardships and triumphs to life.

The main building displays mock-ups of a pioneer home, general store and schoolroom. Six outbuildings include a slaughterhouse, pioneer church, and sheds housing a huge assemblage of agricultural machinery and implements.

Two museum specialties should be mentioned. One is the collection of over 300 pressed-glass decanters and vases, most from 1870 onwards. The second is the display of dozens of century-old, hand-coloured lithographs.

The museum has built a wide reputation by organizing an exceptional program of year-round special events. These include a heritage quilt show, antique auto rally, Christmas craft sale and a celebration of the returning swans (thousands of whistling swans and other waterfowl stop on the shores here during March migration). Thanks to the enthusiastic participation of people from nearby farm towns, these events have a genuine country-fair atmosphere.

Pinery Provincial Park and the Lambton Heritage Museum offer a full day of activities for any visitor. And Grand Bend, the town that offers everything from shopping to sky-diving, is only a few kilometres away.

Pinery Provincial Park
Camping April-November
Winter use December 1-March 31
(519) 243-2220

Lambton Heritage Museum
Monday-Friday 10:00-5:00
Saturday, Sunday &
Holidays 11:00-5:00
Closed Weekends November-February
(519) 243-2600

12 BAYFIELD
City Comforts/Country Charm

Apricots in brandy....lacy lingerie....Cowichan sweaters....breathtaking sunsets....cool river rapids....sandy beaches. Only Bayfield offers daytrippers the best of both Bloor Street and the Great White North.

One of the greatest of Bayfield's city comforts is the shopping, for not only is there an interesting variety of shops, but there is a noticeable absence of cheap, "touristy" places. Bayfield's Main Street stores are strictly first-class in merchandise as well as in historic architecture. There are far too many shops to list completely, but here's an idea of the diversity.

There's Avanti-Leser, with a wide selection of works from Ontario's best-known potters, functional kitchenware, fine art in ceramic and stoneware, and one of the best collections of glass art you'll see anywhere. The Potting Shed sells cut flowers, silk flowers, bird feeders and gardening accessories; the beautiful garden here is welcome relief for shoppers' feet. Gallery Indigena specializes in fine art and clothing fashioned by Native artists from across the country.

Bayfield has some exceptional women's clothing stores, with all the best in knit sweaters, suits and elegant casual wear. And even though Main Street is only a couple of blocks long, it has two shops which sell Victorian-style lingerie: Renaissance Lace and Under the Skin. Bayfield also has shops for the active person. Sharkskin Weathergear specializes in marine and expedition clothing and gear. And so no one in the family goes out of style, No Kidding sells the best in fashion for the younger set.

After shopping for the very best in clothing, art and antiques, only the very best in food will do. The selection of dining rooms in Bayfield almost eclipses the selection in shopping. At one end of Main Street is the Albion Hotel and its adjacent deli and gourmet food shop. At the other end of Main Street is the charming Little Inn, with its giant willow tree and wide two-storey veranda. The Little Inn has been in the hospitality business since 1862, when it was a stagecoach stop on the London to Goderich route. The ambitious menu is famous for luscious desserts. Main Street is also home

Little Inn, Bayfield

to the Red Pump Restaurant, with one of the best reputations in southwestern Ontario. A word to the wise: Bayfield's food does not come cheap.

For a chance to sit quietly away from the tourists, try the lovely little garden of heritage perennial plants in the front yard of the Country Bakery and Cafe, which is a good place to find a wholesome, inexpensive meal.

With all the attention being paid to Main Street shopping, it's easy to forget that Bayfield started out as a harbour and mill town. There are marinas on both sides of the harbour; find them by finding the lakeshore and following the streets downhill. As with uptown, the marinas in Bayfield are out of the ordinary. No more speedboats, but row after row of yachts and the best in sailboats. A sand-and-pebble beach near the marina is the best place to watch the sunsets that made the region famous.

There's another tourist draw in the Bayfield vicinity that shouldn't be overlooked. The Benmiller Inn at Benmiller offers world-class accommodation, dining, and a recreation area hidden among the green hills of Huron County. From Bayfield, drive along County Road 31 to Highway 8; drive west (in the direction of Goderich) until the Benmiller signs at County Road 1 (about 6 1/2 kilometres south of Goderich); from the turn, it's three kilometres to the Benmiller Inn.

The hamlet of Benmiller was once a thriving woollen mill and flour mill town. A large measure of genius has gone into the transformation of the two mills into a hotel complex. The rugged nature of the original buildings is retained in the hotel's fireplaces and huge exposed beams. Best of all, the mill equipment has been recycled in the form of lamps, table tops, chandeliers and clocks. Even humble flour sacks have been used as curtains. The Benmiller Inn must be seen to be believed.

The kitchens at the Benmiller Inn have a legendary reputation, drawing customers from all over the province and the United States.

As with the restaurants in Bayfield, these are not meals for the budget-conscious.

The recreation facilities at the Benmiller Inn are for the luxury of hotel guests only and are a drawing card on their own. In winter, there's cross-country skiing and skating. The rest of the year enjoy swimming, biking (bikes provided free to guests), fabulous hiking, fishing, jogging, and a games room with billiards and table games. The best of city life and country life combined.

The charm of Huron County — the verdant river valleys and fresh air — can be enjoyed without spending a lot of money. Follow signs in Benmiller to the Falls Reserve Conservation Area. There are almost 100 hectares of nature to ramble at Falls Reserve, but the main draw is the Maitland River. There is a long series of rapids here that are tailor-made for wading on a hot day. Small pools of water between the rocks warm up to create a multitude of natural bathtubs. And the more adventurous can try body-surfing down the entire length of the rapids.

Bayfield and Benmiller are perfect opportunities to sample an assortment of city comforts in a setting of country charm. Spoil yourself and experience Huron County today.

Falls Reserve Conservation Area
April-Thanksgiving:
Daily until dusk

Most shops and restaurants
open daily in summer; many
close for the winter.

13 GODERICH
Sunset Strip

Ontario's suncoast, that strip of sand and turquoise surf from Grand Bend to Sauble, is notorious for towns that have sold their souls to make holiday dollars. But Goderich stands apart from them all, with the dignified character befitting the centre of government and society life in Huron County. Goderich is one of those daytrips that has the right stuff: a good combination of history, pleasant strolling and, of course, the beach.

Make the first visit of the day the Huron County Historic Jail, at the corner of Highway 21 (Victoria Street) and Gloucester Street, in the north end of town. This is one of Ontario's most unusual tourist sites.

If anything would have deterred crime in early Huron, it would have been the imposing appearance of this jail, with its massive walls rising five metres above ground and buried two metres below, to a thickness of almost a metre. An unusual octagonal design (like the town plan) is uninterrupted except by a single door and long, dank entrance corridor. Your tour by brochure is a solitary one.

An 1842 courtroom occupies the rooftop cupola. A record of offences and sentences hangs on the wall. It lists a 25-cent fine and a month in jail for vagrancy, the most common reason for imprisonment. The lower storeys of the jail are organized into cell blocks, three cells to each "arm" of the octagon. Each cell is a dreary concrete cubicle measuring approximately 200 centimetres by 2 metres. Metal bed frames were the only furniture. There were no mattresses provided, and one prisoner complained that marks on his back from the bed frame and springs took five days to disappear. And to think that this was considered advanced prison design!

The central block of the jail contains the laundry, kitchen, jailer's apartment, day rooms for socializing, doctor's office, and bathroom. The standard menu is posted: breakfast of bread, potatoes and coffee; dinner of bread, salt beef, potatoes and molasses; supper of porridge and molasses. (Luckily, there are better eating options in Goderich today.)

Attached to the jail is the governor's house. What a contrast to walk through the door from the peeling plaster of the jail into Edwardian comfort. There's a copy of the text of an interview between governor and jailer regarding the causes of crime in Huron County. The conclusions are interesting. It was thought that confining youthful offenders with hardened criminals, alcoholism and overcrowding in jails contributed to criminal activity. Some things never change.

After the dreary jail, refresh your senses with the marvelous view of the Maitland River valley and Goderich harbour. Step across Gloucester Street to the top of the cliff and feast your eyes. If the jail's corkscrew staircases work up your appetite, Robindale, next to the jail, is a beautiful older home with gourmet food. And downtown there's the Hotel Bedford on the "Square," newly renovated, with an extensive menu featuring local fish.

Goderich is fabulous for walking, with street after shady street of immaculately kept older homes. One of the nicest streets is North Street, just a block west of the jail. North Street is also the location of the Huron County Pioneer Museum.

A museum tour begins with a 25-minute film on the hardships of pioneer life in Huron County. Each of the galleries in the museum delves into a different facet of life in the region over the last 150 years. These include military life, occupations, domestic life, transportation and agriculture. The museum is amazingly spacious, with galleries large enough to contain a reconstructed main street (some of the storefronts are authentic, having been moved from neighbouring towns), an old train engine, and two complete windmills. Although this is a museum and not a pioneer village, it is certainly the most thorough treatment of life in early Ontario you'll find anywhere.

The remainder of the day can be spent on the Goderich waterfront, part beach and part port. (Follow West Street to Harbour Street, dropping in at aromatic Cuthbert's Bakery en route.) The grain elevators and the towers of the Sifto salt mine dominate the view, and the harbour is busy with trucks, trains and Great Lakes ships. One is reminded at every turn that Goderich has been a major Great Lakes port since its very beginning. The wheelhouse of a 1907 lake freighter, the *Jay C. Morse*, sits near the beach and houses a collection of historic photographs of Great Lakes ships and other nautical memorabilia. The parking lots are delineated by authentic anchor cables and marine ropes.

Town Beach is at the foot of Harbour Street, and larger St. Christopher Beach is further along the waterfront; they are connected by a boardwalk. Both beaches are beautifully sandy and have lifeguards during the summer. Town Beach is the home of Captain Fat's, with a well-deserved reputation for good beach cuisine — chips, sandwiches, burgers and lots of fresh fish. During the summer, there are boat cruises of the harbour, weekday afternoons from Salt Mine Road and weekend afternoons from the Town Beach.

Goderich is well known for its glorious sunsets, and locals will inform you that *National Geographic* magazine declared this the best sunset-viewing spot in North America. Best of all, if you're very fast, you can catch the last rays twice: once from the main beach and a second time from the top of the bluff behind the beach. Simply drive up the hill to Cobourg Street and along to Lighthouse Park. Or walk along the road towards Christopher Beach and scamper up the narrow staircase leading to the bluff.

Sunset, Goderich

Goderich citizens work hard to keep their city deserving of the title "the prettiest town in Canada" (given by Queen Elizabeth). Come and judge for yourself — and don't forget to see the sun set twice!

Huron Country Historic Jail
Victoria Day-Labour Day:
Daily 9:00-4:30
Labour Day-November 30:
Monday-Friday 10:00-4:00
Saturday & Sunday 12:00-4:00
(519) 524-6971

Huron County Museum
May-Labour Day:
Monday-Saturday 10:00-4:30
Sunday 1:00-4:30
September-April:
Monday-Friday 10:00-4:30
Closed Saturday
Sunday 1:00-4:30
(519) 524-2686

Huron County Marine Museum
May-September:
Daily 1:00-4:30
(519) 524-2686

14 BLYTH
Blyth Spirit

For those who have been turned off theatre festivals by high prices, traffic and restaurant waiting lines, take heart: there's an agreeable surprise waiting in Blyth. To urbanites across the province, Blyth may indeed seem a trifle out of the way. Nevertheless, in the 13 seasons since its founding, Blyth productions have received the highest praise from critics and patrons alike, and Blyth touring plays have been successful in theatres across the country.

The Blyth formula? Specialize in Canadian plays, run programs of workshops for writers, performers and technicians, and set the highest of standards for theatrical and commercial success. Many theatre-lovers think that Blyth is simply the best thing to happen in Canadian performing arts in years.

The Blyth Festival runs mid-June to mid-September, and there are often concerts, children's programs and art events during spring and fall. Prices are about one-third or less that of the "big" festivals. Contact the box office, order tickets for an evening or matinee performance, and plan on a day in and around Blyth, enjoying the charm of Huron County's small villages.

Blyth is well known as one of Ontario's last tannery towns. Shoppers have been faithfully travelling to Blyth's two factory outlets for leather, sheepskin and wool products for years. Bainton's Old Mill is located on Queen Street, just north of the downtown. The building is an authentic mill, and the tannery business began here in 1894; the operation is run by the fourth generation of the founding family. Bainton's specializes in processing lambskins, which produce a higher-quality leather and wool than sheep or cattle hides.

The Old Mill is located a couple of kilometres south of Blyth on Highway 4. This is the larger of the two outlets and offers more European-made high-fashion items.

There is a wide variety of products at both outlets: leather and suede coats, pants, gloves and purses; woollen sweaters, coats and ladies' suits; sheepskin jackets, mitts and moccasins; fur and felt hats; and wool blankets. And there are fabrics, sheepskins and leathers for crafty people.

There are other stores in Blyth to keep you busy until theatre time. Don't miss a visit to The Pottery, just across the street from Bainton's. All ceramics and stoneware are produced on site and include functional kitchenware and lamps. The decorative plates, each with a unique bouquet of local wild-flowers, are out of the ordinary. For stained-glass lamps, windows and gifts, visit the Station Glass Works on Dinsley Street, just east of the downtown.

A wander around town will introduce you to Christmas and Country on Queen Street, with a large selection of decorations, wicker, pillows, rugs and wall hangings. Remember When... on Dinsley Street West is a tiny shop selling tiny things; if you have an aunt or grandmother to buy for, head here for soap, candles and miniatures. There's a shop selling fine art and theatre items in the basement of Memorial Hall (which houses the Blyth Festival).

Strolling around Blyth can be addictive: it is quite simply one of the friendliest places to visit. The hospitality is unfeigned, as is the local pride in the theatre. On a theatre night, most of the countryside comes into town to see the plays, and you can catch the small-town atmosphere as locals discuss drama along with the weather.

The success of the theatre has led to a boom in good dining. The most convenient place is in the basement of the theatre, where lunches and dinners are served during the two hours prior to showtime. The menu isn't extensive, but it is eclectic. The Blyth Inn, at the corner of Queen and Dinsley, has

Country roads

has one of Ontario's best-preserved nineteenth-century downtowns; and Belgrave has a trout hatchery where you can try your luck with rod and reel.

The Blyth spirit is so infectious, you'll be wanting to spend a night in the area. There are more bed-and-breakfasts and old inns than can be named. Pick up a listing at the tourist information booth on Dinsley Street West.

Once bitten by the Blyth spirit, you will be returning often for a taste of culture Huron County style.

country fare and lots of homemade desserts. The Blithe Spirit Tea Room on Queen Street serves teas and light meals in a century house, or on the patio. Farther afield is the famous Benmiller Inn in Benmiller, and Bayfield with its Little Inn, Albion Hotel, and Red Pump Restaurant. An old favourite with patrons and performers alike is Bartliff's Bakery and Cafe in Clinton, on Highway 8 south of Blyth, which features home cooking, a delicious array of specialty baked goods, and terrific sweets at unbeatable prices.

One could easily spend a day in Blyth, but there are a number of nearby communities that are also worth a tour. If you pass through Clinton, don't miss the School-on-Wheels in Sloman Park. This railway car is still outfitted as a schoolroom, just as it was for decades while visiting remote communities in Northern Ontario. (It was the subject of a Blyth production.) Even if the school is not open, you can get a good look through the windows. Brussels, to the east of Blyth, has a pretty mill dam and stream turned into a municipal park; Seaforth

Blyth Festival Box Office
(519) 523-9300
(519) 523-9225

School-on-Wheels
mid-May to mid-October:
Monday-Friday 2:00-5:00
Saturday, Sunday & Holidays 1:00-7:00
(519) 482-9583

15 LONDON
A Walk on the Historic Side

Among the pleasures of touring southern Ontario are the leisurely strolls through our many towns and cities that have well-preserved Victorian neighbourhoods. The last half of the nineteenth century and the first decade or two of the twentieth were marked by the rapid accumulation of wealth, and Ontarians were only too eager to display their success by building mansions. These homes were designed according to a variety of European styles, modified by local conditions and tastes, to create a unique Ontario architecture.

London is a superb place to study our heritage of stone and brick, since it has within a small area examples of every residential form popular in Victorian Ontario. This fortunate circumstance allows us to survey eight decades of architectural history in a few hours.

The best place to begin is at Eldon House, built in 1834 and home to four generations of the Harris family. The house is of frame construction, one of the few buildings in the area to survive the fire of 1845 which destroyed most of early London. Plain, symmetrical, and built around a central hall, Eldon House combines Regency and Georgian styles.

Eldon House presents a rare opportunity to see a historic home with most of its original furnishings intact. The dining room is set for an elaborate dinner, appropriate for the centre of London society life. A back hall is filled with a mix of items only the Victorians could assemble: African hunting trophies, a human skull, and a grandfather clock. It's a treat to poke through the kitchen cupboards (circa 1929), a refreshing change from the typical "hands-off" policy of most

Eldon House

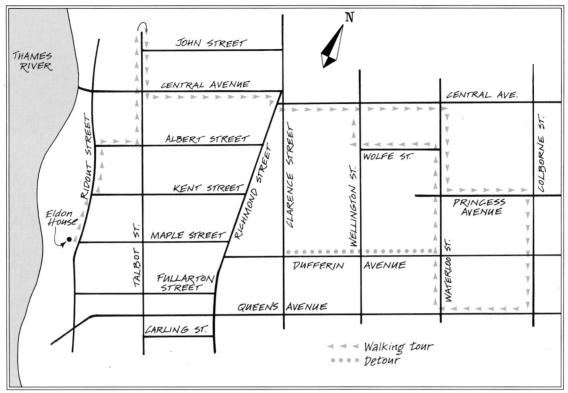

London

museums. And don't miss touring the grounds; there's an excellent period herb garden and a remarkable view of the Thames River Valley.

Eldon House is the most convenient place to purchase *The Historic Heart of London,* source for much of the architectural details for today's walk. Head north on Ridout Street. The first home of interest is one of the most contemporary on today's tour, number 565, built in 1910. By contrast, 76 Albert Street was built in 1865. This was the home of London *Free Press* founder Josiah Blackburn. It is constructed of local white brick and illustrates the typical Georgian form: a central front door with a window on each side and three balanced windows on the second storey. It is interesting to compare these first two houses to see how design principles have been altered to suit early and mid-Victorian tastes.

A contrast to these homes are 90 Albert Street and 585 Talbot, both in the Italianate style fancied by many Londoners. Italianate homes are bright and airy, with many long,

narrow windows. Wide eaves and scrolled brackets are also diagnostic features.

Number 607 Talbot is worth a special look. It is one of the few representatives of Ontario cottage architecture on today's walk. The extensive use of gingerbreading and the single central gable identify the style as Gothic Revival.

The next group of houses take a little extra walking to see, but they are surely worth the effort, for they are London's grandest architectural relics. Number 639 Talbot, a Neo-Gothic house built about the time of Confederation, was home for a time to George Harris of the Eldon House family. Its neighbour, "Firebrae," built in the 1870s, has been the residence of the Bishop of London since 1912. The porch and entrance, modelled after a Greek style, were added to a simple Georgian house.

Numbers 651, 653 and 661 Talbot are good examples of homes typical to the London upper-crust. "Locust Mount," 661 Talbot, was the home of Elijah Leonard, foundry

39

owner, mayor, and senator. Number 651 (built circa 1905) was the home of the McCormick family of cookie fame.

This is a good point to break for a meal, since there are three appropriate eateries nearby. The Toddle Inn, 640 Richmond, was a blacksmith's shop from 1893 until 1947, and it has been a restaurant ever since (closed Sunday). The decor and menu are twentieth-century diner, but the food is pleasingly fresh. Villa Cornelia is a beautiful Queen Anne house at 142 Kent (closed Sunday). A little further away, the Marienbad at 122 Carling is in a well-restored building which was the original office of the London *Free Press*. The food is Central European (closed Sunday lunch).

And now on to the second phase of the historical house tour. You will notice several contrasts from the earlier walk in the Ridout and Talbot Street area. The area of London east of Richmond is of more recent construction, generally post-1870. There is a greater variety of architectural styles, and more flourish in the use of ornamental wood and stonework. The houses and grounds are generally on a smaller scale, as we explore a more middle-class area.

We begin at Central Avenue and Richmond Street, with a wonderful group of mansions along Victoria Park's northern edge. Just as the grandest homes of the Ridout area were positioned along the Thames Valley, so the best families of the rising middle-class vied for a home site close to the park. The houses on Central were built in the 1880s and 1890s. Number 256 was occupied by the Labatt family until 1975.

Heading south on Waterloo Street, there is a riot of architectural styles to study: Queen Anne, Italianate and Romanesque, to name a few. Marvel at the coherence of the streetscape, despite the jumble of turrets, gables, bay windows, archways, gingerbreading and mosaic roofs.

The stone arches of 300 Princess are typical of the Romanesque Revival style popular in the late 1800s. Because of the emphasis on

256 Central Avenue

massive, formal stonework, this form was usually restricted to large public buildings. The southeast corner of Princess and Waterloo features a line of restored late-Victorian terrace houses, today's only representative of a style very common in old London.

It's a good walk to two immense homes, 468 Colborne Street (1903) and its neighbour, 400 Queens Avenue (1909). Number 468 Colborne was one of the largest homes in London at the time of its construction. It is loaded with features loved by Victorians, such as a round turret, a generous porch, and lots of stained-glass windows. Number 400 Queens is a study in exterior decoration: every bit of it, including the spiny roofline, has been used as a surface for ornamentation of one type or another.

Waterloo Street just north of Queens is a virtual design catalogue. It is one of the best places in London to enjoy the height of Victorian architectural caprice, as owners opted for an eccentric mix of styles. An early piece of urban renewal, 471 Waterloo was built in 1910; it is identified as Classical by the columned front porch. Numbers 478 and 484 show their age by their Italianate design (1876 and 1875, respectively). Number 478 was originally Italianate in style but was completely redesigned with the columned front popular in the late 1800s.

As you come to Dufferin Street, you many want to detour west to the corner of Clarence, and the rectory of St. Peter's Church. Although not strictly within today's topic of domestic buildings, this is the only chance to see the mansard roof of Second Empire design. Even though the rectory was built in 1870, the growing penchant for embellishment had taken hold, evidenced by the use of eave brackets and stone at building corners.

Back to Waterloo Street and numbers 496 and 502, beautifully preserved Queen Anne homes. Popular during the last decade of the nineteenth century, this form is distinguished by round turrets, gambrel or steep gable roofs with patterned tiles, and stonework around windows and doors.

Perhaps the most pleasant part of the walk is along Wolfe Street, which is little changed since the turn of the century, when it was an area of comfortable middle-class homes. It's a lovely leafy scene in summer, and just as interesting in winter, when there's an unobstructed view of the buildings.

The last block of this tour is along Wellington Street, where only three grand homes remain to remind us of what this area would have looked like when Victoria Park was completely framed by the best that money could buy in nineteenth-century London.

During a winter visit, the rink in the park is a lovely place to skate, the swirling skaters providing a kaleidoscope of colour. In summer, this is a good place to rest your feet before returning to your car and the twentieth century.

Eldon House
Daily, year-round: 12:00-5:00
Closed Monday
(519) 661-5165

16 LONDON
A Day for the Kids

Daytripping is a great way to holiday with children. The little ones can stay on their normal schedule, sleep in their own beds at night, and don't have to spend too many hours in the car. Instead of having your kids follow you from one adult attraction to another, head for London, where there are several terrific places designed especially for children.

The adventure begins at the London Regional Children's Museum. It is located on Wharncliffe Road near the Thames River. For travellers on the 401, exit at Wellington Street and turn west on Commissioners, or exit at Highway 4 (Lambeth) and follow Highway 4 west to Wharncliffe.

The name of the game at the Children's Museum is activity; this is not a place for the timid. Three floors of exhibits encourage children to touch, see, smell, taste and hear their way into the world of science. Each gallery has exhibits geared to the abilities and interests of all ages, from tot to teen. This is Canada's first children's museum, and it is one of the few suitable for the very young. Even the lab demonstrators and craft leaders are youthful, drawn from the ranks of local science students.

Probably the most popular area is the cave, where kids can crawl in the world of bats and stalactites. "The Street Where You Live" is an exploration of traffic control, fire-fighters, bus drivers, and underground wiring. The museum has an area devoted to Inuit culture, with parkas to wear, soapstone to carve, and traditional bone and antler games to play. There are also galleries dealing with physics, the body, computers and astronomy, to name but a few topics.

The museum is a beautiful adaptation of a 1915 school. A three-storey glass atrium is always filled with children, parents and grandparents working on craft projects related to the theme of the week, which may vary from dinosaurs to Father's Day. Just outside the atrium is a small amphitheatre and garden. The garden is designed to be seen, smelled, and touched. As with the rest of the museum, the garden is wheelchair accessible.

After exploring the museum, children will be ready for the imaginative outdoor playground. Unique wooden sculptures are part art and part gym, as kids run, jump and swing on boats and a variety of creatures. The stroller set might be content to take a ride on the pathway along the river, which is accessible from the playground.

The rest of the day can be spent in Springbank Park, where there is an afternoon full of activities for kids. Bring your brown-bag lunch and drive or bike south on

London Children's Museum

Wharncliffe one block to Horton, and hence to Springbank Drive. Travel westbound and you can't miss the park. The most convenient parking is near Storybook Gardens, although on summer weekends people arriving later in the day may have to park a little further from the action.

Most people think of Storybook Gardens when they think of Springbank Park. This collection of fairy-tale statues, gardens and animals is best for the very young, although the adventure playground portion will interest older kids as well.

Springbank Park has a host of other activities more suitable for the entire family. On a warm summer day, there's nothing like a river cruise. The *Tinkerbelle* has 20-minute and 90-minute cruises, the shorter probably being better for young children. The cruise leaves every 30 minutes, travelling upstream past large numbers of geese and ducks, and a historic pumping station. The longer cruise, leaving twice daily, makes it to the forks of the Thames in downtown London, where passengers may disembark for a few minutes. If self-propulsion is more your style, rent a pedalboat, canoe or rowboat, also available at the *Tinkerbelle* dock. Life jackets and other equipment are provided.

Right beside the *Tinkerbelle* dock is an old-fashioned merry-go-round that appeals to all ages. And while you're munching on hot popcorn from the snack cart, take a ride on a horse-drawn tram that makes its way through Springbank Park. Catch the tram, the least expensive ride going, at the entrance to Storybook Gardens.

If your young charges have still more energy to wear off, try a game of soccer or frisbee on the acres of lawn in the park, feed the geese the last crumbs of your picnic, or visit the Raynor Rose Garden at the corner of Springbank and Wonderland Road.

After all this activity, the young ones (and the older ones) will be ready to return home, quite satisfied with a day all their own.

London Regional Children's Museum
Monday-Saturday 10:00-5:00
Friday 10:00-8:00
Sunday and Holidays 1:00-5:00
(519) 434-5726

Storybook Gardens
May-September:
Daily 10:00-8:00
Labour Day-Thanksgiving:
Daily 12:00-5:00
(519) 661-5770

Tinkerbelle Cruises
June-Labour Day: Daily
20-minute cruises every half-hour
10:00-5:00 and 7:30
90-minute cruises 11:00 and 5:00
September & October (weather permitting):
Saturday & Sunday only
(519) 473-1095

17 LONDON
The Good Life

One of the most common messages in the media today is that we must adopt a healthier way of life. A common formula prescribed for the good life is wholesome food, fresh air and fitness. Visit London, where this wholesome prescription can also be fun.

For the food part of your new regimen, visit Covent Garden Market at King and Talbot streets. Although the building is modern, the tradition of a market at this site is as old as the city. Nineteenth-century London had several markets, and this particular market became the city's most important in 1846, when public-minded citizens donated the site to the city.

Covent Garden is not a typical farmer's market. First of all, the hours are set for the convenience of shoppers, not vendors: six days a week from early in the morning until 6PM, Fridays until 7PM. Secondly, there is a range of international and gourmet food items here that have never seen a farm. It's more like a classy food fair than a conventional farmers' market. At Covent Garden you can sample tzatziki, adzuki beans and nori at one location!

If you're the type that likes to keep up with food fads, then this is the place to browse and ask questions, or buy culinary gifts for the hard-to-shop-for. There are fruit and vegetable vendors with the conventional supply of onions and cabbage, but also carambola and purple basil. Displays sparkle with jars of herb vinegars and apricots in Napoleon brandy. The varieties of cheeses and sausage must number in the thousands;

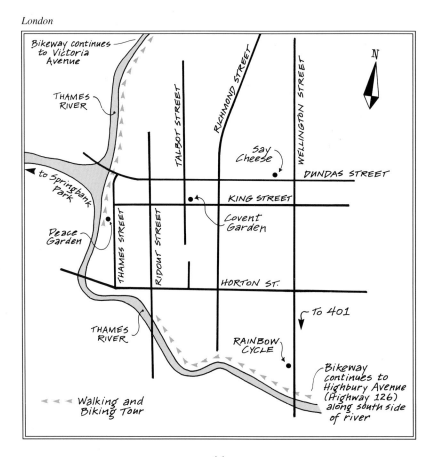

London

they come from Germany, Hungary, Holland, Italy, Australia, Greece. The scent of herbs and spices warms the air throughout the market, emanating from a corner stall with bulk and packaged savouries from around the world. There are also craft shops and ethnic food stores at Covent Garden, and a snack bar offering health food.

Try not to go overboard on the generous samples of meat and cheese the vendors hand out, for there's a special place for lunch nearby. It is an easy walk, so leave your car at the market. Say Cheese (closed Sunday) is a restaurant that takes cheese very seriously. The restaurant has a pub atmosphere and offers a wide menu featuring cheese in most dishes, from soup to dessert. Say Cheese also serves unusual potables (alcoholic and non-) from around the world. The basement shop markets cheese and breads of highest quality. Knowledgeable staff are ready with suggestions and advice on how to buy, store, cook and serve cheese. A visit to Say Cheese will fortify you for the fresh air and fitness part of the day.

London is blessed with an abundance of parks, paths and bikeways. Bring your own bike, or rent one from Rainbow Cycle and Sports at 101 Wellington Street. The cost of renting a bike is outrageously low. If biking isn't your favourite method of self-propulsion, the paved paths throughout London's parks are just fine for running or walking as well as biking.

If you decide to bike, head south from Rainbow Cycle along Wellington to the south branch of the Thames River. The bikeway is on the north side of the river. At this point, the river's edge is left a natural tangle of trees, shrubs and wildflowers. The path ends near Horton Street, and the daytripper must follow sidewalks for a short distance along Horton and then north along Thames Street to the Peace Garden. Walkers and daytrippers with their own bikes might start this tour at the Peace Garden.

The Peace Garden is a good vantage point for viewing the Middlesex County Courthouse, the grey castle to the northeast. The courthouse was completed in 1831, apparently modelled after Malahide Castle in Ireland. Next to it is the London Art Gallery, housing over 2,200 Canadian and international works.

From the Peace Garden northwards, the pathway is clear for pedestrians, bikers, roller-skaters and skateboarders north to Victoria Street. Ambitious hikers can continue from there on the Thames Valley Hiking Trail all the way to St. Marys. It's exhilarating to get up some speed on a bike, and you can on these pathways: most pathway users tend to go west, towards Springbank Park, leaving the north Thames pathway fairly uncluttered.

The scenery alternates between urban wilderness and manicured parkland, with the wide Thames always in view. Along the way there are gyms for children and fitness stations for the whole family. Just north of Oxford Street there are washrooms and drinking fountains for the thirsty weekend athlete. You might want to stop here to watch the skateboarders on the public skateboarding ramp; there are even bleachers.

North of Victoria, the path is simply packed earth, but it is still suitable for biking. Continue along as far as your legs will carry you. Don't forget to allow for the return trip to your car or to Rainbow Cycle to return the bike.

We may have to return to the workaday life tomorrow, but we can be glad that we took at least one day to sample the good life in London.

18 LONDON
A Tale of Two Settlements

Communal living quarters...single-family housing; fortified site...undefended site; subsistence agriculture...family farming and small trades. The story of early Ontario's Native and European settlements couldn't be more different. London is unique in that among its attractions are two re-creations of historic settlements. Taken together, the Lawson Pre-historic Indian Village and the Fanshawe Pioneer Village offer an intriguing opportunity to compare two Ontario ways of life. But today's trip needn't be all study, since there is ample occasion for fishing, picnicking and hiking.

The Lawson site (and the neighbouring Museum of Indian Archaeology) is a little tricky to find. Take Highway 22 to Wonderland Road and drive south. Or take Highway 4 to Wonderland Road and drive north. Follow signs on Wonderland Road just north of Gainsborough for the Museum of Indian Archaeology.

At the Museum of Indian Archaeology, there are over 40,000 artifacts illustrating 10,000 years of developing Indian culture in southwestern Ontario. The museum is not solely concerned with artifacts, but with the science of archaeology itself. Any mystery buff will be intrigued by the piecing together of a community's food, housing, clothing and even religion by a methodical study of its physical remnants. The arduous tasks involved are explained in detail: surveying, soil analysis, bulldozing, shovelling, trowelling, screening, reading soil stains, gathering fragments, reconstruction and study. Some hands-on exhibits even let us *be* archaeologists, as we search through pottery, open storage drawers and handle tools.

It's time to step into the Lawson Pre-historic Village and see the results of years of research. The village is on a bluff overlooking the Medway Creek and is the actual location of a Neutral Indian village that 500 years ago was home to several hundred people. The tall palisades, defence platforms and reconstructed longhouses are located as close as possible to their original sites. Step inside a longhouse, complete with hearths and sleeping platforms, on a day when few other visitors are about, and you get an eerie feeling that you are not really alone. Outside, there are garden plots with traditional crops of beans, squash, corn, sunflowers, and tobacco. Informative display boards interpret village life.

As with the museum, the village explains the science of archaeology. During summer months students from the University of Western Ontario dig and sift through the site, discovering pottery and other remnants daily. You can even try your hand at it yourself!

Drive north on Wonderland Road, east on Highway 22, south on Clarke Sideroad and hence to Fanshawe Conservation Area. Then head for the Pioneer Village.

The scene shifts dramatically from the Lawson Indian Village, as this settlement represents life in a small crossroads community of the Thames Valley. Most buildings have been moved to this site; some are replicas. Fanshawe may not be one of Ontario's largest pioneer villages, but it is probably one of the least crowded, which gives it an authentic small-town atmosphere. It also means that you feel free to ring the fire bell, sit at school desks, and watch the livestock without rushing.

There are over 20 buildings, including rough log houses and barns, a Presbyterian church, Orange Lodge, schools, fire hall, frame houses and storefronts. Of special interest is the logbook in the general store; it is always open to today's date of a century ago so that we can ponder what we would have been doing in pioneer days!

Regular features of Fanshawe Village include costumed guides, demonstrations of pioneer skills such as candle-making, weaving and smithing, farm animals to pet, and special-event weekends with period foods, wagon rides, games and music.

Fanshawe Conservation Area is a cornucopia of activities for year-round fun. There's camping, swimming and picnicking, for starters. (Picnicking is recommended for today's trip.) Fanshawe has an excellent maze near the entrance to the Pioneer Village. Man-made Fanshawe Lake is 6 1/2 kilometres long; there's a boat ramp (no motors, please), and boardsailing instruction and rentals. During the winter, there are 15 kilometres of groomed trails, ski and snowshoe rentals and instruction, horse-drawn sleighs on special-event weekends, and ice-skating on the lake. The staff at the park entrance are happy to help you choose your activity, and they have plenty of schedules and maps to help you navigate.

Why not spend some time at Fanshawe engaging in one of the few activities common to inhabitants of both settlements we studied today? Fishing. Fanshawe attracts scores of fishermen year-round. During the summer, try your luck from boat or canoe, or from the small fishing docks. Or join most natives and find a comfortable seat on the shoreline of Fanshawe Lake or downstream from the dam. Fanshawe is the site of a major walleye (pickerel) transfer project, so fishing should be productive. There's also ice-fishing when conditions are suitable.

For an even surer chance at catching dinner, try the Cedarbrook Fish Market on Fanshawe Park Road near Highbury. Bring your own equipment and enjoy Cedarbrook's pond stocked with rainbow and speckled trout. There are fish to be caught all season, but spring and fall will keep you hopping. Don't like to clean your catch? Cedarbrook will, as well as sell you trout, salmon, and a netful of other species.

This daytrip has been a unique chance to try our hand at being archaeologists and early settlers. As for surviving in our own hectic culture, a day spent in London's two historic settlements helps us return with renewed appreciation for our modern conveniences and abbreviated working hours.

Museum of Indian Archaeology
April-November:
Wednesday-Sunday 10:00-5:00
December-March:
Wednesday-Sunday 1:00-4:00
(519) 473-1360

Fanshawe Conservation Area
May to mid-October and
December to mid-February:
Daily 8:30-4:30
Otherwise Monday-Friday 8:30-4:30
(519) 451-2800

Fanshawe Pioneer Village
late May to late September:
Daily 10:00-4:30
September to mid-December:
Monday-Friday 10:00-4:30
(519) 451-2800

19 PORT STANLEY
Port Stanley Revisited

We daytrippers are not a new phenomenon by any means. Our parents and grandparents were keen weekend adventurers, and some of their favourite resort villages remain for us to enjoy today. One such destination is Port Stanley, a Lake Erie fishing village 64 kilometres south of London on Highway 4.

Port Stanley is the consummate daytrip, with beaches, country trails, shopping, bird-watching, historic sites, boat cruises, and an antique railway. The delights of Port Stanley begin even before you leave the car, because the view of the colourful harbour and the town set on the steep sides of the Kettle Creek Valley is an enchanting surprise.

Start your day by wandering the harbour area, watching fishing tugs and yachts manoeuvre in the tight confines of the harbour. Be sure to end your ramble along the east side of the harbour in order to take in the Port's most interesting shopping area, along Main Street. Most stores are in recycled wharf buildings and historic homes and carry a nautical theme, which makes the atmosphere more maritime and less touristy.

Main Street is anchored at each end by Port Stanley's best-known tourist attractions, the Kettle Creek Canvas Company and the Kettle Creek Inn.

The Kettle Creek Canvas Company was born in 1971 when native Mellanie Stephens began retailing cotton clothing of rugged and practical design. This cottage industry has proven so successful, despite the upscale pricing, that Kettle Creek Canvas now has several dozen stores nationwide. The firm's flagship store, housed in an 85-year-old fish-processing plant and warehouse, is one of the highlights of the Main Street strip. A beautiful renovation job has turned the frame warehouse fashionable grey outside and natural pine inside (closed Sundays).

Although the Kettle Creek Inn was built as a private home in the 1840s, it was converted to a hotel in the 1920s, evidence of the Port's appeal as a resort town even at that early date. Careful renovation blends the original elegance of the home with an unassuming wood exterior in harmony with the Main Street scene. The Kettle Creek Inn

Port Stanley Terminal Railway

has a wide reputation for local fish expertly prepared, and as a bonus, in warm weather dinner is served in a garden pergola amidst a lush backdrop of lilies and roses.

Main Street supports another fish eatery, Jackson's Wharf, where you can eat while watching the harbour action in a three-storey warehouse that has been dramatically modernized.

After lunch, you may want to take in another attraction, the Port Stanley Terminal Railway. The London-Port Stanley line was built in 1856 to carry freight, but by the middle of this century, daytrippers were the main cargo. Our predecessors came here from London to picnic on the beach or to swing to Guy Lombardo at the Stork Club. Disuse and disrepair threatened the line, but railway enthusiasts rallied to repair the railbed and tracks, and the London-Port Stanley carries tourists once again, although now only as far as nearby Union.

The rolling stock here is not of interest to the average traveller; a diesel-electric engine pulls a converted freight car and caboose. (The original massive and elegant beauties that carried Port-bound partyers are better viewed at Halton County Radial Railway, see trip 37.) It is the rail line itself that is important here as we continue to follow the trail of daytrippers of yesteryear.

The trains depart from the terminal near the King George Lift Bridge where Kettle Creek enters the harbour. The tracks follow Kettle Creek, passing moored pleasure craft and suburbs before heading out into farmland. This area has been producing tobacco since the 1920s, so the fields here look much the same as when grandpa and grandma took the family to the beach.

Passengers may disembark at tiny Union. The one-room station has a display of photographs on the history of the London-Port Stanley line. Although the pace is not exhilarating, it is certainly a pleasant way to spend 50 minutes.

After returning to the holiday atmosphere of Port Stanley, the daytripper has the delightful dilemma of deciding what to do next. For many it will be a visit to Port Stanley's main tourist draw, Big Beach. It is at the south end of William Street, the first southward turn east of the Lift Bridge (at the gas station). There are washrooms and parking, and a long boardwalk at Big Beach. Another beach, Little Beach, is at the end of Main Street; there are privies and parking at Little Beach as well.

There are other attractions in Port Stanley: the *Delta Queen,* a reproduction riverboat, gives tours of the harbour on afternoons from May to September; Hawk Cliff, a few kilometres east of town on the Lake Erie shore, is a good place to observe birds of prey during fall migration in late September; a pamphlet describing a walking tour of historic buildings is available at the town hall and from local merchants.

Like our ancestors, we leave pretty Port Stanley hot, sandy but happy holidayers, looking forward to our next visit.

Port Stanley Terminal Railway
May & October:
Saturday, Sunday & Holiday afternoons
June-August:
Tuesday-Sunday
November-April:
Sunday afternoons
(519) 782-9993

Most shops and restaurants
open Tuesday to Sunday

20 SPARTA
Sand in Your Shoes

Who could guess that one of the best places to race down a hill, and a soft sandy one at that, would be on the flat countryside along Erie's north shore? To convince yourself, drive east from Port Burwell 12 kilometres to Sand Hill Park, a privately-run family picnic area, campground and beach.

The sand hill is over 135 metres high, a unique natural feature created by southwesterly winds. The Indian pottery and arrowheads discovered nearby indicate that the site has been attracting attention for some time. The hill was the site of an American observatory used to survey and chart Lake Erie. Tourists began paying to visit the huge sand hill during the late 1800s, at 10 cents a visit. The cost of visiting Sand Hill Park may have escalated a tad, but it remains one of the most intriguing natural features in southwestern Ontario.

The hill is quite an invigorating climb, especially on the steep landward side, so take the path of least resistance, found at the southeast corner of the park. The path leads through a small valley shaded by poplar and maple. A beautiful vista of Lake Erie opens up, framed by rising sand hills on either side, the narrow beach far below your feet. Take advantage of the strategically placed bench to take in the fresh air and marvelous scene, and then continue the descent to the water. (You'll appreciate the bench even more on the way up.)

After your Lawrence of Arabia struggle to walk up and down the sand hill, head for one of the best beaches in Ontario, perhaps the country. Take County Road 42 west to Port Burwell Provincial Park. The beach is pure sand (not a pebble!), over 2,000 metres long and very wide. It is so large that it's not crowded, even on summer weekends, so it's easy to stake a claim to a spacious portion of sand. On a hot day the breezes off the lake act like a cool balm. The water is shallow enough to wade a great distance in, although on rough days there may be an undertow. The rear portion of the beach has trees large enough to cast good shade.

Port Burwell Provincial Park offers camping, hiking trails (the park is habitat to marsh birds such as bittern and to rare ferns), biking on interior roads, and fishing. The incessant winds make for good windsurfing and kite-flying. The town of Port Burwell is also good for biking, the pier is popular for fishing, and there are several restaurants serving local fish. The most significant feature of Port Burwell is the 1840 lighthouse, one of the oldest in Canada. Visitors may, for a small fee, climb to the top for a view of the town and harbour.

If all the swimming and climbing has you ready for lunch and a change of pace, head for tiny Sparta. Drive west on County 42, (also called Highway 73 and County Road 24), then turn north at County Road 36 and drive about three kilometres to Sparta.

Sparta must be one of Ontario's most unspoiled villages, and it's worth at least half a day of exploring. Almost all the buildings date to the last century, when Sparta was a Pennsylvania Quaker settlement.

First things first. Head for The Sparta House Tea Room, with simply the best scones anywhere, always oaty and hot. The menu also includes an interesting variety of light meals. This building was originally built as a hotel around 1844 and has a charming clapboard exterior with double-decker veranda. The building also houses the British Shop, with everything from woollen ties to Dandelion and Burdock soft drinks. Kitty-corner from the Tea Room is the Pedlar Shop. It has a wide range of decorator items for babies and kids, as well as women's clothing and local craft items.

Renowned artist Peter Robson has a studio and gallery next to the tea room, in two

Peter Robson Galley, Sparta

renovated buildings. Robson creates lovely watercolours of landscapes and historic towns in southwestern Ontario. The gallery is in The Abbey, a former girls' school and inn, built in 1840 and beautifully restored.

Across the street is Roseberry Place. The building is part of the attraction: weathered board-and-batten with a false front. Roseberry Place sells antiques and reproductions such as rocking chairs, rag rugs and decoys. Half-a-kilometre to the west is Spartan Antiques, with an excellent selection of antiques and gifts. But the treat here is the high-quality reproductions, authentic in every detail, including milk-paint and linseed-oil finishes.

In the front yard of Peter Robson's studio stands a map indicating historic sites in and around Sparta. Village merchants are happy to provide a tour brochure, which can be the basis for a day of exploration. There are several buildings here you won't see elsewhere; for example, an active Friends (Quaker) meeting house with separate entrances for men and women, a house built

entirely of cobblestone, and two buildings built of adobe.

This has been a great trip for those long, lazy days of summer: sand, surf and serene Sparta.

Sand Hill Park
May-Thanksgiving:
Daily 8:00-11:00
(519) 586-3891

Port Burwell Provincial Park
mid-May to September:
Daily 8:30-dusk
September-May:
gate closed, but walk-ins permitted
(519) 874-4691

Most Sparta shops and restaurants open Tuesday-Sunday during the summer, weekends only during the winter.

21 ST. MARYS
Stonetown

Here's a recipe for an unbeatable daytrip. Take a pretty valley at the confluence of the Thames River and Trout Creek; add one of Ontario's largest concentrations of historic stone buildings; season with country inns, refreshing quarry waters and shops geared for the tourist. What do you have? St. Marys, protected from the ravages of commercialism by its position slightly off the beaten track, and yet in the heart of a countryside beloved by daytrippers.

Start your tour of Stonetown, where it all began, on the river near Queen Street. One hundred years ago, this part of the Thames supported over a dozen grain, lumber and woollen mills. The fine stone home facing the river on the north side of the bridge belonged to mill-owner William Hutton during the 1850s and 60s. A walk through the remains of Hutton's front gardens, between the house and the mill race, is like stepping back in time. We soon emerge onto the river flats where generations of

townsfolk have quietly sauntered. The Victoria Bridge on Queen Street is one of many bridges and viaducts of architectural or historical merit in St. Marys.

Head to the corner of Queen and Water streets, one of Ontario's most attractive intersections; it is rare to find a major crossroads where such beautiful stone buildings sit on all four corners. Mac-Pherson's Craft Store marks the site of St. Marys' first store; the original log building was replaced by stone in 1855. The Hutton block on the southwest corner dates from about 1854. Together these buildings provide a good picture of how Ontario main streets appeared a century ago.

Much of the commercial core along Queen Street was constructed in the mid to late 1800s. The highlight of the downtown is the Andrews building; it has been a home to jewellers, and only jewellers, since it was built in 1884. While most of St. Marys is

St. Marys

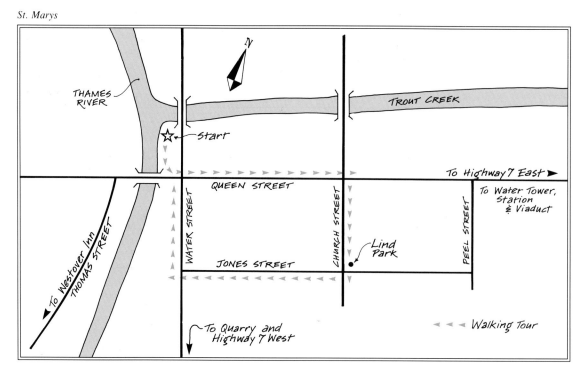

Town Hall

rather plain and unpretentious, the jeweller's is a piece of Victorian whimsy, from clock tower to pastel paint. Another notable storefront is that of the McIntyre Drug Store; the historical plaque notes that it has been perfectly preserved in every detail, including windows and doors.

Timothy Eaton and brothers operated a dry goods business in what is now Hubbard Pharmacy. In 1869, dissatisfied with the barter system used by local farmers, they left for Toronto and a merchandising empire.

St. Marys offers tourists some interesting shopping. The Perth Country Gallery (149 Queen) sells original art, including lovely sketches and paintings of historic St. Marys. St. Marys Antiques (21 Water) sells British and Canadian glass, silver and artwork. Canadian folk art is featured at the Gaggle of Geese (167 Queen) and The Touchmark Shop (31 Water).

The Town Hall, at the corner of Queen and Church streets, is St. Marys' pride and joy. Constructed of local limestone, the hall was completed in 1891. The style, known as Richardson Romanesque, gives an air of massive grandeur, with lots of arches, towers and turrets. The hall has served at various times as a butcher shop, police lockup, and dance hall.

Turn away from the river and walk uphill (always uphill in St. Marys!) into a residential area that was home to many of the merchants instrumental in creating the lovely streetscape along Queen.

At Jones and Church streets is shady Lind Park. The Linds, founders of St. Marys Cement, owned the home at 51 Church Street. The town walking tour, available from most merchants, notes that from the entrance to Lind Park one can see four of the most prominent buildings in town. The towers of Holy Name of Mary Catholic Church and the Presbyterian Church are across the valley to the north. (St. Marys, with its large contingent of churches, is filled with the sound of bells on Sundays.) In the foreground are the towers of the Town Hall and the Andrews building.

At 224 Jones Street is the house of George Carter, grain magnate. (In its heyday, St. Marys shipped more grain than any other Ontario centre, including London and Toronto.) With typical Victorian domination, Carter had his son James and son-in-law H.L. Rice build grand homes nearby, the former at 67 Peel Street South and the latter at 236 Jones Street. Both homes were designed by William Williams, a local architect responsible for the MacPherson block, the Andrews building, the Church Street bridge, and scores of other projects in town. No other individual influenced the appearance of St. Marys to such an extent.

Head back down Jones to Water Street, where two more masterpieces in stone await.

The Opera House, looking like a medieval castle, was the hub of social life in early St. Marys. This was the place to see celebrities of the day, from John A. Macdonald to the Marx Brothers. Across the street is the Post Office of 1907.

St. Marys has many other architectural gems for the avid walker. These include the water tower (in use from 1899 until 1987, an American Waterworks landmark); the Queen Street train station (1907); the St. Marys District Museum on Tracy Street; and the Grand Trunk London and Sarnia viaducts.

The hills of St. Marys will have daytrippers panting for refreshment. There are four choices for those wanting to have lunch or dinner in a historic building: Sir Joe's in the Post Office; the Opera House Restaurant; the Creamery, on Water Street just north of Trout Creek (good river views); and elegant Westover Inn.

Westover was the retirement home of millers and merchants William and Joseph Hutton,

Church Street bridge

who built many of the buildings in the Queen and Water Street area. Westover Inn sits amid nine hectares of parkland, with cross-country skiing, swimming and other guest facilities. Westover has a reputation for elegant accommodation and haute cuisine. The grounds include a shrine from Westover's years as a seminary; the Marion Shrine is Canada's only garden mound, an artificial hill used for surveying the landscape.

If you are wondering where the stone for building St. Marys came from, it's time to find out. Drive south of town on Water Street to "The Quarry," advertised as Canada's largest natural swimming pool. The water is deep and cool. There are diving boards for every taste and skill, as well as change rooms and a snack bar. Because there is no shallow end to a quarry, there is no suitable swimming for young children.

St. Marys has everything a daytripper loves — outdoor activities, dining, history, and it is an easy drive from theatres in Stratford, Blyth and London. Don't be surprised if Stonetown becomes a regular habit.

St. Marys Quarry
Public Swimming
May-August:
Monday-Friday 1:30-dusk
Saturday & Sunday 10:00-dusk

22 STRATFORD
Much Ado About Something

Stratford is Ontario's premier daytrip destination. But too many people roar into town, take in a play, and roar out again. Put a sense of adventure into your next visit to Stratford. Take potluck on rush seats for the Festival or Avon theatres, or be even more adventuresome and give the performers-in-training at the Third Stage a try. You can use the tremendous savings on tickets to enjoy a potpourri of Stratford offerings.

One possibility is to take in a medley of antique and fine art shops. Begin the day in the hamlet of Shakespeare, a few minutes east of Stratford on Highway 7. Many tourists have yet to discover the unaffected hospitality of Shakespeare, which extends to a supply of umbrellas waiting at the entrance of each store: in case of rain, simply grab one and leave it at the next port of call.

You can find early Canadiana at Kathleen's Antiques, Peter C. Land and Antiques Canadiana. There is surely an old wardrobe or cabinet to fit every taste and budget. Formal Victorian furnishings and an impressive collection of china and glass are featured at Glen Manor Galleries. Also for the serious collector is Jonny's Antiques. Much of the porcelain and glass at Jonny's dates to the eighteenth century. Don't miss the shop speciality, Victorian calling-card cases in tortoise-shell and mother-of-pearl.

Shakespeare is more than antiques. It's Christmastime at Chanticleer. There are enough trees, garlands, toy soldiers, wreaths and ribbons to keep you decking the halls for a decade. The British royal family takes centre stage at Upstairs Downstairs in plates, antique photos, magazines and Victorian collectibles. There's also a large collection of aviation prints.

Head west to Stratford. Just after entering town, stop to take in a few shops on Ontario Street. Yesterday's Things has a large selection of used books; Canadian Arts has a commendable collection of paintings, prints and wood etchings; Penny Farthing sells furniture as well as china and glass; and there are more glass, lamps and carpets at Paul Bennett Antiques across the street.

Try your hand at brass-rubbing in the basement of Knox Church at Ontario and Waterloo streets. There are over 60 replica brasses (large memorial plaques from medieval churches) from Britain and Europe. The brasses are likenesses of well-known figures, as well as humble folk, children and animals. Assistance is available for visitors trying their hand at rubbing for the first time. Ready-made rubbings, swords and suits of armour are on display.

The next stop, tiny York Street, is hidden behind Wade's Flowers, towards the west end of Ontario Street. Peel back the centuries at Gregory Connor Antiques, where some of the furniture dates back over 200 years! At Props, the displays are pure theatre: jewellery, sculpture, puppets, and prints with a performing arts theme. Gallery 96, across Lakeside Drive, sells the work of regional artists.

York Street is a good base for exploring Stratford. At the tourist information office, there are washrooms, menus from local restaurants, and metered parking. And this is the place to board the boat for cruises on Victoria Lake. There are small boats and canoes for rent as well.

Before leaving York Street for more shopping along Ontario Street or in the centre of town, take an appreciative look at the 1887 Perth County Court House, just around the corner on Huron Street. Between the Court House and the river are the Shakespeare Gardens.

When the town bustles with sightseers, this can be a tranquil retreat. A long border of perennials spills over with all the traditional

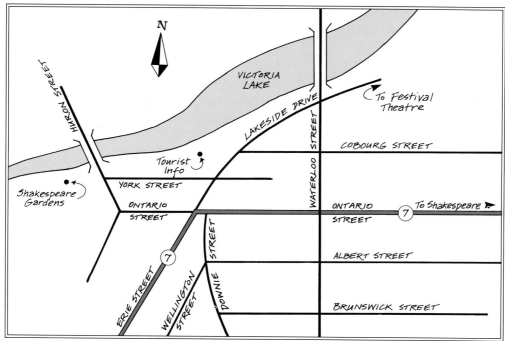

Stratford

favourites: peony, rose, day lily, iris, poppy. A central herb garden is home to plants commonly grown in Shakespearean times: hyssop, yarrow, anise, pennyroyal, sweet woodruff, and their kin.

On a fine day, a picnic is called for: the 70 acres of parkland around Victoria Lake is one of the prettiest picnic spots in Canada. Prepared repasts can be ordered from the Leslie Cheese House (on Highway 7 at the west end of town), or from Delicatessen Stratford Packers (Wellington Street downtown). If you are in town on a Saturday, you can put together your own picnic at the Stratford Farmers' Market, at the fairgrounds. While picnicking near the lake, take in Art-in-the-Park, an outdoor exhibition that runs Wednesdays, Saturdays and Sundays from July through September.

Stratford is surely one of Ontario's best restaurant towns. The problem lies in having to choose just one restaurant. Reservations are recommended during the busy Festival season. The Church Restaurant, on Waterloo Street, serves haute cuisine at haute prices, but the setting, in an old church complete with coloured windows and organ pipes, is very special. Ever heard of bats in the belfry? At The Church, there's a bar in the belfry. Stratford residents also recommend Rundles (9 Cobourg) and The Old Prune (151 Albert) for elegant and imaginative cuisine.

Stratford is appropriately home to a number of good English-style pubs. Most renowned is the Queen's Inn Pub on Ontario Street. This building and its various additions have been dispensing food and friendly accommodations for almost a century and a half. More recently, the Taylor and Bate Brew Pub has started selling its own lager, to very positive reviews.

There is much more to busy Stratford than just theatre; enough, in fact, to make it a very pleasant destination any time of the year.

Stratford Festival Box Office
(519) 273-1600

Most shops and restaurants open daily

23 INGERSOLL
More Cheese, Please

Ontarians are among the world's biggest cheese lovers. Every man, woman and child in the province eats about 10 kilograms of cheese annually. The heart of Canada's cheese industry is Ontario; we are responsible for about one half of our nation's total cheese production. And the heart of Ontario's cheese industry lies on the fertile green hills between Kitchener and London. Today's daytrip takes us into those hills for some investigative cheesing.

Begin the day by lunching at the Elm Hurst Inn. It is conveniently located at Highway 401 and Highway 19 North in Ingersoll. Elm Hurst was built in 1872 for the James Harris family, pioneers of the local cheese industry. This is a picture-postcard country home from the top of its Gothic gables to the inviting wicker furniture on the porch.

Although the Harris family no longer resides at Elm Hurst, they would be pleased with the gracious welcome accorded guests. It's like visiting an elderly (wealthy) aunt. There are fifty guest rooms in an addition which so closely matches the original home in colour and style that you'll be challenged to find exactly where the two buildings meet.

You needn't be an Inn guest to enjoy dining at Elm Hurst. Especially recommended are the lunch and Sunday brunch buffets. The buffets begin with seafood and end with an extravagant dessert table filled with dozens of choices in cakes, tarts and mousse. The Harris family, with all their success, couldn't have had it so good.

An après-lunch ramble around the grounds is called for. The carriage house has been

Elm Hurst Inn

converted into two floors of fine arts and crafts. The collection represents the best in regional craftsmanship, with pottery from Thamesford, paintings from Sparta and Waterloo, and sculpture from the Six Nations Reserve. Occasionally there are guest artists on hand to meet the public. The gallery also sells clothing and collectibles.

At the north end of the Elm Hurst grounds is a historical plaque describing the infancy of Ontario's cheese industry. The first factory was founded on the Harris farm in 1865. Local producers used a gigantic Cheddar cheese as a marketing ploy. The cheese, weighing over 3,300 kilograms, was a metre high and 2 metres across. It required 45 yards of cheesecloth for wrapping. The cheese was exhibited at the New York State Fair and the World's Fair in Britain. A 135-kilogram slice was returned to Ingersoll to allow the participating dairy workers a taste.

Drive into Ingersoll from Elm Hurst. Follow the signs to the Cheese Factory Museum in Centennial Park. This modest board-and-batten building is a replica of a typical Oxford County cheese factory in the nineteenth and early twentieth centuries. Early machines and tools are used to illustrate each step in the production of cheese: weighing milk, separating cream, adding rennet, draining the whey, cutting the curd, adding salt, pressing the curd, cutting and storing the cheese. There's also a 20-minute video filmed at a local factory. Visitors will find a map indicating locations of old cheese factories of interest; at one time, there were scores in the Ingersoll area alone.

The day would not be complete without picking up a few packages of local cheese. There are several options, depending on how far you wish to drive. If you visit on a Saturday, there is the Ingersoll Farmers' Market downtown. There are two cheese shops south of Ingersoll near Highway 19. The first, the Village Cheese Mill (open daily), is in Salford, an old cheese-factory town. There are over 50 kinds of cheese offered, including 12 kinds of Cheddar. Much of the cheese comes from Tavistock. The store has a country general store feel, and also sells confections, local jams and honey. Further south, near Tillsonburg, is the Wedge Cheese House (open daily). Watch for roadside signs indicating an eastward turn. With over 90 varieties of cheese, as well as meats and frozen foods, the Wedge is very popular. Pine River cheese from Ripley, near Kincardine, is a special item here.

There are two bona fide cheese factories in the Ingersoll area. The largest is the Tavistock Cheese Company (closed Sundays) at Tavistock, on Highway 59. The selection will baffle your taste buds; good thing the prices allow for several purchases. Tiny Uniondale, on Highway 19, is home to Uniondale Cheese (closed Sundays). The accommodating people at Uniondale have provided a window into the processing area so that curious visitors may watch the proceedings. Monday through Thursday mornings, the counter staff are willing to explain the factory activities.

As you drive home, wave gratefully at the black-and-white Holsteins you pass. They are responsible for the neatly wrapped brown packages on the back seat. Bon appetit!

Elm Hurst Inn
Monday-Saturday 12:00-2:00 and 5:00 onwards
Sunday 10:30-2:00 and 4:00-8:00
(519) 485-5321

Ingersoll Cheese Factory Museum
May, June, September & October:
Saturday, Sunday & Holidays 1:00-5:00
July & August:
Daily 10:00-6:00
(519) 485-4930

24 NORWICH
Flower Power

Although the back-to-the-land movement has waned, it has left a legacy of reawakened interest in gardening and nature study. The traditional distinction between these two activities is blurring as Canadians, like the early British landscapers, are finding "that all nature is a garden." This daytrip combines nature walks and garden tours in a celebration of flowers.

Today's botanical adventure begins just west of tiny Sweaburg. Trillium Woods Nature Preserve is a wildflower sanctuary established to protect our provincial symbol, the white trillium. At first glance this appears to be a rather ordinary Ontario woodlot surrounded by farmland, and a rather small woodlot at that. But it only takes a brief walk along the trail to make one realize that this is an extraordinary place.

For those who think of the white trillium as three graceful white petals with three large green sepals underneath, a marvelous treat is in store. At Trillium Woods, trilliums sport green stripes on white petals, purple stripes on green petals, or even entirely green petals. The short trail is best walked in May, when the trilliums are in full bloom; they are joined by May apple, jack-in-the-pulpit, foamflower and other spring beauties.

Just across the road from the park is Jakeman's Maple Products, where spring is heralded by pancake breakfasts served February through April. Tours of the sugar bush are also conducted. Maple products are sold year-round and are a sweet souvenir of what is known locally as "The Trillium Bush." The Jakeman store is the original post office from the town of Sweaburg, and locals have been gathering and gossiping on these worn wood floors for well over a century. The friendly country atmosphere is the most authentic you will find anywhere.

The Tea Rose is just west of Highway 59, about four kilometres north of Norwich. A florist specializing in silk flowers now offers tea and light snacks on a 130-year-old farm. The focus of the tea room is a formal pool and fountain. The room is bedecked with silk flowers of all types; some even float in the pool. The renditions of spring crocuses and daffodils are particularly realistic. The shop includes a Christmas room, craft and art gallery, imported food corner, and floral design supply area.

Norwich and surroundings

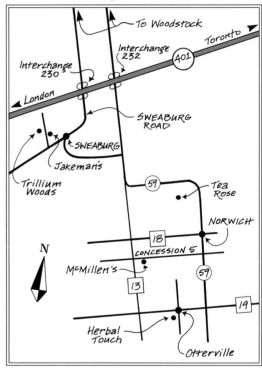

Return to Highway 59 and turn south to Norwich. Between the Bakery and Bun Shop and the Norwich Deli, you can piece together supplies for a picnic lunch. Head west through Norwich along County Road 18 and turn south on County Road 13. There are signs for McMillen's Iris Garden at Concession Road 5; the farm is one kilometre along.

During the iris season, from mid-May through June, there is enough beauty here to drive a gardener mad. The McMillen family grows bearded irises, Siberian irises and day lilies. The bearded iris is appropriately nicknamed the "rainbow" flower, and the growing fields are dappled with lilac, sky blue, apricot, delicate pink, gold and burgundy. Don't miss studying McMillen's lush gardens for good ideas on arrangement of form and colour. They even have a water garden for their Siberian irises and other plants which prefer wet feet. Although you'll want to buy several plants, the best idea is to return home with a McMillen order form; the plants will be sent UPS when the time is best for them to be uprooted.

Head east to Highway 59 and then south. Turn west on Oxford Road 19 and drive a couple of kilometres to Historic Otterville, as locals refer to their village.

The final botanical visit of the day is The Herbal Touch. It is located at 30 Dover Street, just south of Main Street (Oxford Road 19). Marilyn Edmison-Driedger welcomes visitors to wander through her magically scented garden brimming with plants for parlour, kitchen and boudoir. A small barn houses a treasure-trove for gift-hunters and herbalists alike: wreaths, bouquets and brewing pots for the decorator; uncommon books on gardening and herbs; lemon eucalyptus for the teapot and thyme for the stewpot; homemade vinegars and oils. Open houses held annually in June and December include samples of herb bread and rhubarb-nectar punch from Marilyn's own recipes.

Tranquil Otterville is well worth a tour. At the west end of town, on Main Street, is Treffey's Mill. Built in the mid-1800s, it is one of the oldest continuously operated water mills in Ontario. The grassy grounds offer peaceful picnicking. Another interesting spot, just to the west, is Woodlawn, an eight-sided house now used as a community centre. A good place for a stroll is Otterville Park, reached via a footbridge from the north end of Dover Street.

The daytrip officially ends here, but it is worthwhile to explore the countryside around Norwich a little longer. While spring has been most richly announced at Trillium Woods, McMillen's and The Herbal Touch, the whole area has a vibrant air. By taking time to see the orchards in blossom and to hear birds noisily settle boundary disputes, we are assured that spring is here to stay.

Trillium Woods Nature Preserve
Daily, year-round

Jakeman's Maple Products
Monday-Saturday: 9:00-5:00
February-April: Sunday 10:00-4:00
(519) 537-8863

The Tea Rose
April-January:
Tuesday-Saturday 10:00-5:00
Sunday 12:00-4:00
(519) 424-2255

The Herbal Touch
May-December:
Tuesday-Saturday 10:00-4:00
Other times by appointment
(519) 879-6812

McMillen's Iris Garden
May & June: Daily
(519) 468-6508

25 SIMCOE
Tobacco Road

A drive in the countryside is a favourite pastime for many Ontarians. Farm country is not only picturesque, it also has an air of stability that is lacking in cities. But appearances are deceiving, and agricultural methods constantly change as different crops and practices develop. And what changes farming changes the landscape of Ontario.

Today's trip, a rural tour around Simcoe, in the centre of tobacco country, is best taken August through October. The visitor will find out about tobacco growing and some of the crops considered alternatives to tobacco, and will explore pretty Simcoe, the town that tobacco built.

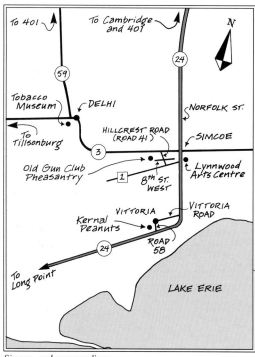

Simcoe and surroundings

Drive to Delhi on Highway 3. Just west of Delhi's downtown is the Ontario Tobacco Museum. This spacious model of a pack barn contains a thorough explanation of tobacco growing, curing and packing, complete with historic and modern-day implements. The countryside scene suddenly

starts to make sense: greenhouses to lengthen the short Ontario growing season; kilns for curing; barns for stripping and packing cured leaves; sheds storing equipment for planting, spraying, irrigating and harvesting.

The museum also presents the development of the modern tobacco industry in Canada through historic photographs, newspaper clippings and interviews. Displays show the development of various tobacco marketing agencies that led to greater market and price stability for producers.

Agriculture changes with society, and tobacco production is in decline. For an inside look at some of the crops that might be successful alternatives to tobacco, drive towards Simcoe along Highway 3. En route stop at Zelem Farms for blueberries, ready-picked or pick your own. The berries are wonderful and the prices very low.

Follow the map to find the Old Gun Club Pheasantry on 8th Street West. The Pheasantry welcomes visitors, but please phone ahead.

The Pheasantry raises up to 10,000 pheasants a year for restaurants, as well as for the store on the premises. The season starts in early May, when day-old chicks arrive in their new home: recycled tobacco kilns. Although the Pheasantry did not start out as a tobacco farm, this does seem like a tailor-made use for unused kilns, since young chicks need accurately controlled humidity and temperature. From the kilns, the birds move outside to about two hectares of flight pens planted in rapeseed, sunflowers and sorghum. It's fun to watch the pheasants disappear into the rapeseed as you approach. The Old Gun Club tour operates from May to September, but the best time to see mature ring-necked males in all their colour is late August and September. There's an opportunity to buy frozen birds and attractive Christmas boxes at the end of the tour.

Drive on to Simcoe. Simcoe is one of rural Ontario's wealthiest towns, and it shows. Norfolk Street, Simcoe's main drag, is lined with large trees and even larger red-brick homes on spacious grounds. In the centre of town, on Colbourne Street, is the beautiful courthouse, built in 1864, with its attached jail and library. An elegant residence on Argyle Street, just east of downtown, has been artfully renovated as the Lynnwood Arts Centre. That a small rural town would have a gallery with such high-quality art and music presentations is a testament to the stature and wealth of twentieth-century Simcoe.

If it's time to eat something more substantial than blueberries, have lunch in Simcoe. There's the Conservatory Restaurant on Norfolk Street (closed Sunday lunch). It is a picturesque old home with a reputation for gourmet food. It is not inexpensive, but the adjoining piano bar, Trumpets, is more modest in price and menu. In the shopping mall behind the courthouse there's Christian's for fish and chips.

Sweet Valencia peanuts is another crop with potential to replace some tobacco. The next stop is Kernal Peanuts in Vittoria. Drive to the quiet hamlet of Vittoria, where signs will direct you to the Kernal Peanut plant.

The best time to visit the plant is on weekdays when the machinery is in operation, although tours are given on weekends. In September and October peanuts are harvested and washed in nearby fields. Because Ontario has a short, damp harvest season, conventional methods and machinery had to be made more efficient, very much like the way American tobacco methods had to be adapted to Canadian conditions. Tobacco kilns are used to dry the peanuts, which takes about five days.

Visitors spend most of the tour in the main plant watching elevators and conveyors shuttle nuts to a shelling bank; the shells are used as cattle feed and mulch. The nuts are sorted according to size, each size for a different market: bird feed, candy, peanut butter, table use. Tours also include the peanut butter plant, where the roasting and processing takes two days. Kernal Peanuts has a retail outlet with their own natural peanut butter, packaged nuts and candied nuts in many tantalizing forms.

Tobacco country holds some surprises: pheasants, peanuts and gourmet food. You will return home from today's daytrip with greater appreciation for the changing face of rural Ontario.

Lynnwood Arts Centre
Tuesday-Friday 9:00-5:00
Saturday & Sunday 1:00-5:00
(519) 428-0540

Ontario Tobacco Museum &
Heritage Centre
June-September:
Daily 10:00-4:30
September-May:
Monday-Friday 10:00-4:30
(519) 582-0278

Old Gun Club Pheasantry
(519) 428-1230

Kernal Peanuts
Monday-Friday 9:00-5:00
Saturday 10:00-5:00
Sunday 1:00-5:00
(519) 426-8440

26 PORT DOVER
Perch Awhile in Port Dover

Port Dover, on the shore of Lake Erie, advertises itself as the largest freshwater fishery in the world. The annual catch of smelt, perch, bass, whitefish and other species is valued in the tens of millions of dollars, not to mention the contribution of a very active sport fishery. Yet the perch garner all the attention. In fact, you would think that perch were the only things with fins. Mild and sweet, yellow perch has made the reputation of many a local restaurant; it is the principle fodder for Misner's fish plant at the foot of Main Street; and perch is a choice offering at two waterside fish markets.

The place to begin a tour of any port is at the pier, of course. Head for the East Basin Marina, lying on the eastern side of Lynn Creek. Strolling the piers, adjusting one's pace to the rhythmic rocking of the fishing tugs, is a remarkably peaceful pursuit. It's an unusual treat to see so many working vessels in one place. The East Basin is also home to Bravener's Fish Market, where fresh and smoked fish are available seven days a week.

It's back to the car and over the lift bridge to the western harbour, town dock, public beach and parking. The western pier offers a panoramic view of the Erie shore, and an especially close-up look at a lighthouse. Walking the pier is the only way to survey the techniques and success of local "rod and line" specialists as they ply the waters for — you guessed it — perch.

Harbour Street has an interesting assortment of stores for browsing. As more tourist dollars have flowed into Port Dover, this street has assumed a Florida-like appearance, with sandy front yards and cedar-clad stores selling beachwear by the tonne. But there is plenty here with an indigenous appeal. The Sandalmaker is a good place to find footwear suitable for beach and après-beach, and is an appropriate store for Port Dover since tanneries were important businesses during the last century. The Compass Rose is a must stop. It has a nautical theme and is the place to pick up navigational charts, model ships, and miscellaneous boating paraphernalia cast upon shore, such as old-fashioned cork life-preservers. Harbour Street is also

Boat Building, Port Dover

the location of Port Dover's second fish market, Macdonald's, another good place to pick up a sample of local fish. They will even clean your catch for you in the tiny processing room next door.

Further along the street, in a former net-making shanty, is the Harbour Museum. Just outside the door stands a plaque providing an interesting capsule history of the town. Port Dover is old by Ontario standards, the harbour being in active use since 1800. As you will discover inside the museum, much of that history concerns the lives of ordinary people trying to make a living from merciless Lake Erie — fishing, fish processing, shipbuilding, net-making.

The museum offers a glimpse into a way of life that is little recognized or chronicled, but the artifacts speak volumes. Look over items caught in fishing nets or washed up from the thousands of wrecks gone ashore in the Port Dover area. There are charts showing the location of many of these wrecks, and details of dates and lives lost. Shallow Erie, perfectly aligned with prevailing westerly winds, has a mean reputation. There are many tales of brave fishermen who rescued boats in distress, at their own peril.

The technology of Great Lakes fishing, not much changed from decades ago, is also recorded in the museum. A variety of net types are here to handle, as well as mending gear, net winders, bilge pumps, and a ship's bell and helm. All trades have a distinctive tongue, and fishing is no different. Gimmicks, camels, beetles, all take on a new meaning for museum visitors. After being introduced to life on Lake Erie, step out the back door of the museum to view fishing boats moored a couple of metres away.

The fresh breezes blowing off the lake are sure to whet the appetite. Good thing that Port Dover has restaurants aplenty. At one end of the scale is The Arbor, for take-out burgers and other beach food; the aroma is intoxicating. At the more formal end of the scale is the Erie Beach Hotel on Walker Street, where Friday-night perch dinners are very popular. Callahan's Beach House has

a prime location on the sand, with a wonderful deck for outdoor eating.

After lunch, make a trip to the beach. The town beach, by the pier, is long, wide and clean. There are public washrooms nearby, but little shade. Inexpensive cruises on the *Ferroclad* take in a couple of hours on Long Point Bay and leave on weekends from May to October. The cruises will keep you cool on a hot day. Another cool spot is the old Fire Hall, now the Lighthouse Festival Theatre. From June until September there's a smorgasbord of professional productions.

A stroll up Main Street includes a selection of general stores typical of small-town Ontario. A store of note is Trifles, selling niceties such as sachets and lace napkins for bargain prices. Across the street is Anderson's Antiques, specializing in vintage glass, particularly lighting fixtures.

If a day in Port Dover looks like it will turn into two, consider a bed-and-breakfast. The Port of Call on Main Street was built over 130 years ago by the son of town founder Israel Powell. Otherwise, end your day in Port: pour the sand out of your shoes, make a quick purchase of perch for the barbecue, and take a last, respectful look at cool, grey Lake Erie.

Harbour Museum
May-October:
Daily 10:00-5:30
(519) 583-2660

Ferroclad Boat Cruises
(519) 583-1597

Lighthouse Festival Theatre
(519) 583-2221

27 BRANTFORD
The Red Tile

The famous Canadian cultural mosaic. How much do we really know about the individual tiles making up that mosaic? The education of the typical Ontarian with respect to the "red tile" is especially poor. But today's daytrip, to the Six Nations Reserve near Brantford, is a good way to start improving our cultural awareness.

The Woodland Indian Cultural Education Centre in Brantford is the best place to begin. It is situated on Mohawk Street, at the south end of town. The centre is located next to the Mohawk Institute, a 150-year-old residential school for Indians.

Brantford and the Six Nations Reserve

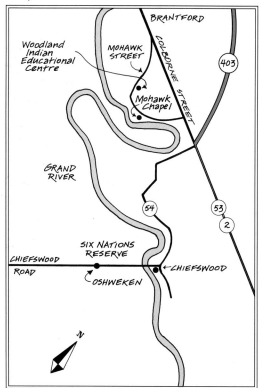

The centre presents a journey through Native history, from pre-European palisaded villages to the present-day Six Nations Reserve. Three-dimensional scenes and local archae-

ological finds illustrate a mature pre-contact society. Life was more than a matter of mere survival: the geometric patterns on pottery indicate that there was time to fashion items of artistic as well as of practical merit. A replica Iroquois longhouse, scene of religious ceremonies and community meetings, has been built within the centre.

The most interesting facet of the education centre is the depiction of cultural transition. Artifacts and costumes make the point that cultural change affected both Natives and Europeans, as customs and technologies were traded along with furs and beads. A study of tools and domestic items is particularly intriguing. Traditional awls, fishing hooks, and axes show a development from indigenous forms to an interesting composite of European and Native methods and materials.

There is an enlightening display on the development of the Six Nations Reserve near Brantford. Land deeds, treaties and photographs describe the relocation of the tribes making up the Iroquois Confederacy from tribal homelands in New York State to Ontario. Further acculturation, such as the establishment of elected reserve councils, is illustrated by artifacts and documents — history never mentioned in schoolbooks, but there in the documents to read.

One of the galleries in the centre, the Indian Hall of Fame, is an education in itself, featuring names and achievements that we should, but do not, identify as Canadian. How many of us recognize the name of Dr. Gilbert Monture, member of a UN Advisory Committee on Israel? And how many realize that Tom Longboat's 1907 record in the Boston Marathon still stands? The Indian Hall of Fame is a record of extraordinary successes in all walks of life: public service, athletics, the military, education.

The second visit of the day is a short distance south on Mohawk Street: Her

Majesty's Chapel of the Mohawks, the only Royal Indian Chapel in the world. Built in 1785 and the first Protestant church in Ontario, the chapel is beautiful evidence of the past status of the Six Nations community. The interior of the simple frame structure is dominated by eight richly coloured stained-glass windows depicting the history of the Iroquois Confederacy in the Brantford area.

Drive east on Highway 53 and south on Highway 54 to the Six Nations Reserve, the largest Indian community in Canada. Near the westward turn for Oshweken, the main village on the Reserve, stands serene Chiefswood, home of Pauline Johnson. Although the home is under restoration and closed to the public indefinitely, one can stroll the treed grounds on the banks of the Grand River. Johnson left Chiefswood as a young woman and went on to become internationally acclaimed as a poet and speaker, championing the cause of her people.

The first stop in Oshweken should be the Six Nations Tourism Office. It's the best place to find out about special annual events on the reserve, such as the Pow Wow in July, Pageant in August, Handicrafters' Bazaar in November, and Snowsnake Festival in January. One can arrange for reserve tours of two to five hours in length. An escort is provided for a small hourly fee, and tours include special events, local foods, historical sites and shops. Alternatively, office staff can give you directions to a number of in-home artists' studios. Many Six Nations painters and potters have achieved international recognition for their work, and reserve roads are dotted with signs advertising art for sale. The tourist office is open weekdays only, a good reason to make Oshweken a weekday trip.

Also on Chiefswood Road in Oshweken is the Two Turtle Studio of Arnold Jacobs. The gallery is devoted to paintings, prints, stone sculptures and antler carvings. Especially captivating are wildlife paintings created by applying several layers of paint by stencil; this makes each painting an original. Don't miss an opportunity to meet with the artist. Jacobs manages to teach about art and the Six Nations without pontificating. His studio is a must visit.

The Village Inn, at the crossroads in Oshweken, seems a typical diner in most respects. But if you are clever enough to plan a visit on Friday, the Village Inn has a Native Day, with local foods such as corn soup, wild rice tarts, pickerel, venison, Indian cookies and strawberry juice. These foods can also be served by special request on other days. The Village Inn is a good spot to survey the comings and goings of a rural community.

The remainder of your visit to the Six Nations area can be spent enjoying the pastoral scenery along the Grand River south to Cayuga and Caledonia (Highway 54), or by returning north to Brantford.

Woodland Indian
Cultural Education Centre
Monday-Friday 8:30-4:00
Saturday & Sunday 10:00-5:00
(519) 759-2650

Chapel of the Mohawks
April, May, June, September, October:
Saturday & Sunday 1:30-5:00
July & August:
Monday-Saturday 10:00-12:00 and
1:00-5:00
(519) 753-4395

Six Nations Tourism Office
(519) 445-4528

Village Inn Restaurant
Daily, closed on Sunday at 2:00
(519) 445-2270

Two Turtle Studio
Tuesday-Saturday 10:00-5:00
Open Sunday during the summer
(519) 445-2014

28 CALEDONIA
Deepest, Darkest Ontario

While the vast majority of southern Ontario residents live in cities or large towns, psychologists and park planners have long argued that people have an innate need for contact with the natural world — trees, water, wildlife. Perhaps that is what makes so satisfying a day in the out-of-doors, discovering what precious pockets of green Ontario remain. A short drive can take the daytripper to places where the concrete jungle seems very remote indeed.

Highway 54 between Brantford and Dunnville along the Grand River meanders through a bucolic landscape. This trip concentrates on the area around Caledonia. About six kilometres north of town on Highway 54 are signs indicating an eastward turn for the Big Creek Boat Farm. Cruises on the Grand River leave several times a day. Each cruise features a roast beef dinner, and some include a nature cruise up Big Creek or a musical revue. Prices are equivalent to the price of dinner alone in most restaurants. The entire cruise facility is wheelchair accessible. Reservations are required.

As commentary from the cruise captain explains, the Grand River is southern Ontario's longest and fastest-flowing river. From its source at Dundalk near Georgian Bay to Port Maitland, the Grand travels 290 kilometres with an average depth of about three metres. An active sport fishery harvests carp, catfish, pickerel, bass, pike and trout.

Big Creek boats travel down Big Creek to the Grand, and then north to the outskirts of Brantford. Most daytrippers will be surprised to find that the shoreline is entirely undeveloped. There are occasional breaks in the trees for sporting clubs, estate homes, cottages, or to create watering places for cattle. The scenery is undramatic but peaceful. There are very few other boaters using the river: the dam at Caledonia restricts the recreational boaters to more southerly portions of the Grand. This fortunate situation means that Big Creek guests are left alone to feast their eyes on the montage of green foliage and brown water, and to hear the chattering of kingfishers.

Some historical detail is necessary to understand why such a tranquil scene remains untouched, when it is less than an hour's drive from the Golden Horseshoe. The lands on both sides of the Grand River were granted to Joseph Brant and the Six Nations in recognition for service on the side of the British during the American War of Independence. Much of the land the cruise passes through is still Six Nations Reserve, protected from the worst of development pressures.

The most northerly point in the cruise is at Chiefswood, birthplace of poet Pauline Johnson, who became internationally acclaimed as a spokesperson for Native Canadians. The view of this handsome Italianate home is largely obscured by trees, but it can be seen by car later on.

Many cruises return directly to Big Creek, while others travel south to Caledonia, and a short walk around the park at the Caledonia dam and old lock station.

If you didn't have dinner on the cruise, drive into Caledonia, where there are several restaurants. You may also want to tour some of the other Grand River towns: Newport, Middleport, York and Cayuga. All have fine Victorian buildings dating to an era of prosperity on the river. Beginning in the 1830s, a canal operated along the Grand, and this spurred development. But the construction of railways meant death for the canal, and just as settlement was expanding elsewhere in the province, Grand River canal towns fell into decline. Only a few small centres remain, as well as some interesting ghost towns.

The serenity of the river will have you refreshed and game for a visit to Killman's

Siberian Tiger, Killman's Zoo

Zoo. Drive north along Highway 6 from Caledonia. At Unity Road, follow signs to Killman's; it is about two kilometres east of Highway 6.

Murray Killman is an artist specializing in wildlife paintings and prints, particularly renderings of big cats, and his 12-hectare farm is home to a large collection of his graceful subjects. Evidence that the cats are kept in first-rate conditions is the fact that several of them have bred and raised young at the zoo — the crowning achievement for any zookeeper. In addition to the jaguars, tigers, leopards, mountain lions and lynx, there are monkeys, elk, bison and domestic farm animals.

Killman's Zoo is in a wooded setting, and the number of visitors is quite small. Wandering along narrow paths, ducking beneath branches, you will come eye-to-eye with a big cat staring at you as only a feline can. With a little imagination, a Killman's visit can take on the feel of a personal safari. Kids love it. Wildlife study at a small private zoo has other advantages over big-city facilities. You can get closer to the animals for a better look, the handlers are always available and eager to talk about their charges, and admission fees are quite low.

The zoo shop sells Killman prints and other wildlife paraphernalia. The artist holds a gallery open house each year in June.

From a cruise on the placid Grand River to a safari near Caledonia, this has been a day in deepest, darkest Ontario.

Big Creek Boat Farm
Late May to October:
Daily 11:00, 1:00 & 5:00
Sunset cruises Friday & Saturday 6:30
Reservations essential
(416) 765-4107

Killman's Zoo
March-November:
Daily 10:00-6:00
(416) 765-4261

29 ST. GEORGE
An Apple a Day

Ontario is apple country. From the time of the earliest French farmers, orchards have been an integral part of Ontario's landscape. Immigrants from across Europe brought their own tree stock, and apple cultivation flourished wherever the Great Lakes moderated the harsh climate. Over the last two centuries many uniquely Canadian varieties have developed as the result of natural processes and horticultural experimentation. North America's most preferred apple, the McIntosh, is an Ontario native; it has proven so successful that it has virtually eliminated much of the competition. It could be called Ontario's agricultural gift to the world.

For some of us, nothing epitomizes Ontario autumn more than a gnarled old apple tree heavy with glossy red fruit. This daytrip is an opportunity to taste the harvest first-hand and to discover a small shopping village with a growing reputation. St. George is located on Highway 5 just east of its junction with Highway 24. The day begins at Orchard Home Farm on Howell Road (one concession north of Highway 5) halfway between Highway 24 and St. George.

Orchard Home Farm makes it easy, inexpensive and enjoyable to capture the authentic flavour of an Ontario fall. Thirty-two hectares of dwarf and semi-dwarf trees provide plenty of picking for adults, while the branches are so loaded with fruit that there's plenty of picking for even the smallest toddler. The fact that visitors can drive their cars right to the trees eliminates hauling heavy baskets of fruit long distances. And even on busy weekends it is possible to find a private nook in the orchard where one can be very much alone to savour the fresh air and the fine fall scenery.

Pricing varies with the type of apple picked, but it is an unbelievably cheap way to buy fruit, about 20 percent of the cost of in-season apples at a grocer's. And at Orchard Home Farm there are varieties you'll never find on an ordinary shopping trip. Gravensteins and Lodis, favourites from over 100 years ago, as well as newer types such as a personal favourite, the Empire, are found here. The diversity of offerings means that there is a long picking season, from mid-August to late October. The older, "heritage" apples from grandmother's day will only be kept in production as long as demand continues, so be sure to leave a spot for these beauties on your picking agenda.

Each apple has a distinctive size, colour, texture and aroma, suiting it for one or two purposes: eating, pies, pickling, jelly, dessert, sauce, or winter storage. Advice on the best apple for your purpose is available from the friendly staff at the orchard entrance; baskets are available for loan or sale, and plastic bags are free to all pickers.

The trees are so productive, and the picking so easy, that you'll have your requirements satisfied in a short while. That leaves the rest of the day for lunch and sauntering through nearby St. George. Once a prosperous town boasting numerous businesses, including a large flour mill, the St. George of today is considerably less hectic, catering largely to daytrippers.

There is a multitude of antique and gift shops on Main Street, each with a good selection of furniture and collectibles, as well as individual specialities. At R-tiques, for example, the specialties are jewellery and fine art, at Ed's they are glassware and oil lamps; and the Old Harness Shop specializes in Canadian primitives. St. George is home to art galleries and studios as well. Among the most noteworthy craftspeople are Donn Zver, east of town on Highway 5 near Troy, and Vaughn Stewart in the Thistlecroft Studio on Main Street. Both potters produce beautiful dinnerware and unusual serving pieces such as pâtè dishes, wine coolers and milkbag holders. A full listing of area shops is available from any of the village merchants. Food can be had at The Gourmette Restaurant, part of Inn St. George, a bed-and-breakfast (adults only), or at Twinklebones Teashoppe. Both locations specialize in hearty British fare such as meat pies and roast beef. Most delightful of all, Twinklebones provides authentic Devon cream teas—a luscious concoction of scones, butter, jam and clotted cream native to southern England.

A summer trip to St. George can include a band concert or flea market on Sundays, or roller-skating on Fridays, all at the community centre. St. George is set in prosperous farm country that is especially pretty at leaf-turning time; you can make a side trip along the local back roads on the way home. Recommended routes are to travel west, past Highway 24 to where the roads become delightfully twisty and hilly, or to travel north on Highway 24, enjoying the most scenic part of the Grand River Valley.

Before leaving St. George, fill your thermoses with pure spring water supplied by an artesian well; a public tap is maintained on Main Street, just north of Highway 5, in the centre of town.

Orchard Home Farm
mid-August to November:
Daily 9:00-dusk
(519) 448-1111

NO-HASSLE APPLESAUCE

20 apples
1 cup water (more required for older apples)

Thoroughly wash, core and quarter or slice apples. Place in heavy saucepan with water. Cover tightly and simmer until tender, about half an hour. Either (1) sieve to remove peel, or (2) puree, including the peel. Test for sweetness and add sugar to taste (about 1 cup sugar for this recipe).

Applesauce can be canned (10 minutes in a boiling water bath) or frozen.
Serve warm or cold with cinnamon and ice cream or yogurt.

30 CAMBRIDGE
Down by the Old Millstream

From its beginning, Cambridge has been a place where things are made. Access to water power, raw materials from an agricultural hinterland, and nearby markets meant that from the early years of the nineteenth century, the towns of Preston, Galt and Hespeler were the locations of many prosperous enterprises. Textiles and clothing, furniture, leather and shoes became local specialties.

The tradition continues, to the benefit of knowledgeable bargain-hunters who scour the factory outlets here in search of the ultimate find. Today we join the pursuit, visiting a few outlets and walking through Galt, a well-preserved nineteenth-century mill town. Galt is a partner with Preston and Hespeler in the Cambridge tri-town.

The thrill of the hunt begins at Cambrian Shoes, the only stop of the day in Preston; it is on Fountain Street at the 401. This is the place to buy footwear for the whole family: runners, casuals, dress shoes, slippers, even safety shoes for both men and women. At Cambrian, there are bargain prices on shoes from local manufacturers such as

Savage, as well as on discontinued lines from retailers such as Eaton's.

It takes a few minutes to negotiate traffic to the Dobbie Drive headquarters of Cambridge Towels, especially if it's a Saturday, but it's worth the effort. This is a real factory outlet, so the small store is not glamorous, but the prices for kitchen, bath and table linens are terrific. Towels, tablecloths, napkins, bath mats, oven mitts and aprons are sold 25 to 75 percent off retail price. For the really budget-conscious, bath towel seconds are sold by the pound.

For the next portion of the trip one can abandon the car and walk between outlets, a walk that includes historic sites and recommended lunching spots. (Notes for today's walk are from a lengthy but excellent walk described in a Heritage Cambridge booklet available from local bookshops and the City Archives in Preston.)

A convenient place to park is Mill Race Park, on the Grand River in downtown Galt. This park combines historic conservation and flood prevention. The remains of the

Mill Race Park, Cambridge

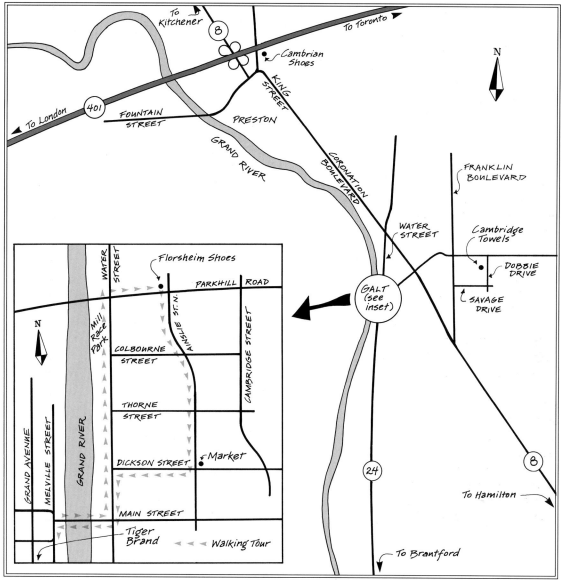

Cambridge

Turnbull Woolen Mill, including stone foundation, millrace and some machinery, have been ingeniously landscaped with an interesting variety of plants, walkways and a small amphitheatre. The park is well worth investigating for the fine views of old Galt and the river.

A block away, at 20 Parkhill Road, is Florsheim Shoes. Have you ever wondered how your neighbour can afford so many pairs of distinguished-looking shoes? He probably shops at Florsheim's in Galt. Top-quality mens shoes in sizes 6 1/2 to 13 are 50 to 75 percent the retail price.

From the corner of Parkhill and Ainslie, walk south along Ainslie. Number 55 Ainslie, Wesley House, was built around 1847 for a cabinetmaker. The style is typical of homes built by the Scots middle class in the middle decades of the last century: close to the road, thick-walled and unadorned.

Wesley United Church (circa 1878) at 49 Ainslie is a substantial granite-and-limestone structure, and is a good introduction to the many examples of masonry you will see today in Galt. Stone was used in the Cambridge area for buildings of all types — public offices, grand homes and cottages

Central Presbyterian Church and the Main Street Bridge

and industrial buildings. These heritage buildings are a testament to skilled local craftsmen and an ample nearby supply of limestone suitable for blocks and mortar. Today's daytripper is much the richer for this fortunate combination.

At Dickson, turn left, past the Cambridge Farmers' Market building. The market has been held here since 1887. Every Saturday this area teems with activity, which spills out of the building and over the sidewalks, as it has done for generations of marketers. You may want to cross to the south side of Dickson to get a good view of the Town Hall, an elegant building of grey granite. The hall was built in 1857, and it is hard to believe that the clock tower was not part of the original structure; it was added in 1897. The Town Hall has been declared a provincial historic site.

At 56 Dickson Street is the old Fire Hall, built in 1898. The large garage doors were replaced by office windows, and if you look through them, you can see the original brass

fire pole. An appropriate lunch spot is 5 Cambridge Street, built in the 1870s as the home of the fire chief. The Sugarbaker's Coffee Shop has a dazzling array of tea cakes, pastries and cheesecakes, all made on the premises in the early hours of the day. Sandwiches are available as well, Monday through Friday. For larger appetites, there's Daisybelle's on Petty Place, the southern appendix of Cambridge Street. A good assortment of sandwiches, salads and sweets are served in a friendly atmosphere.

Backtrack along Cambridge and Dickson, heading towards the river, with the fine front of the Galt Carnegie Library ahead of you. This turn-of-the-century building was designed by Fred Mellish, the same architect responsible for the Fire Hall. Turn south along Water Street and stop at the corner of Water and Main for a glance at the south side of Main Street, where almost a whole block of stone commercial buildings have been well preserved, making it easy to picture this street as it was a century ago. And at 12 1/2 Water Street there stands a building with an eccentric combination of materials and styles, the Old Post Office (1885). Crossing the Grand River on Main Street, one can appreciate why Galt is known as a city of spires. One of the most beautiful is that of Central Presbyterian Church at Main and Melville streets on the west bank of the Grand. The interior of the church is equally interesting, with its curved pews and wonderful stained-glass windows. The street corner in front of the church is a good place to survey Queen's Square, the civic heart of Old Galt. Citizens have stood on the curbs here, and on the balcony of Hume's Block, the stores opposite, to join in commemorating the triumphs and tragedies of a small town.

Now, back to the present, and continue west to Grand Avenue and then south on Grand several blocks to the corner of Cedar. This is the location of Tiger Brand Knitting. (This may be a long walk for some, so you may want to pick up your car to continue the tour.) Well-known locally for sportswear bargains, Tiger Brand was originally established across the river at 36 Water Street South in 1881. Get ready to square your shoulder pads, you may have to fight for your bargains; this place can get crowded. The best deals are in seconds, but look these over carefully.

To recover from the excitement of shopping at Tiger Brand, retrace your steps to the car, at Mill Race Park. If you've left lunch until now, try Haney's at 7 Thorne Street, close to Mill Race Park; there's a wide selection of sandwiches and salads here for eat-in or take-out, so this is a good place for picnic supplies. Otherwise, enjoy a last look at the Grand River, the powerhouse for all that you've seen today, then pack your bargains in the trunk and head for home.

Cambrian Shoes
Tuesday & Wednesday 12:00-5:00
Thursday & Friday 12:00-8:00
Saturday 10:00-4:00
(519) 653-5783

Cambridge Mill Outlet
Monday-Wednesday 9:00-5:00
Thursday & Friday 9:00-9:00
Saturday 9:00-5:00
(519) 623-5520

Florsheim
Monday-Wednesday 10:00-5:00
Thursday & Friday 10:00-9:00
Saturday 9:00-5:00
(519) 621-7211

Tiger Brand Knitting
Monday-Friday 10:00-4:30
Saturday 9:00-3:30
(519) 621-5722

31 KITCHENER
For Shoppers Only

For some of us, shopping is a necessary chore; for others, it is an important form of recreation and even self-expression. But few of us have the time to turn shopping into an educational experience that is also fun. This daytrip does just that, by putting together a tour of factory outlets in Kitchener, city of outlets. As you shop, you learn first-hand about the local industrial base and take an inside look at historic industrial architecture.

Outlets were originally devised by manufacturers as a way of unloading substandard items and ends of lines. But with changes in modern retail markets, outlet shopping is becoming more popular with manufacturers. Factory stores are no longer only for the budget-minded, as well-heeled daytrippers from across Ontario come to cities like Kitchener for a day's shopping.

This trip will follow the route indicated on the map, starting with New Balance Shoes. There are good prices on sports shoes for the family (a limited selection for children), including specialty wear for basketball, soccer, walking, running and baseball. There are terrific bargains on shorts, t-shirts, swimsuits, aerobic suits, and cycling outfits.

The next visit is to Forsyth Shirts on Duke Street. Parking is south of the building. Note that Duke Street is one-way north at this point. The Forsyth family began manufacturing mens' shirts in Kitchener in 1906 and moved to this particular plant in 1917. The outlet store is one of the best. You get a quiver of anticipation just climbing the many stairs, peeking into workrooms in operation as you near the store. There's usually a line-up at opening time, so you know the bargains are worth fighting for.

Pierre Cardin and Forsyth shirts are the main draw here, in all weights, shades, styles and sizes. But there are also lots of ties, socks, sweaters, pajamas, underwear, uniform shirts, and ladies shirts. Prices are very good for seconds and discontinued lines. Sometimes you can amuse yourself by looking for the flaws in golf shirts — logos printed incorrectly or in odd places. It may be the closest some of us get to owning shirts from the more prestigious country clubs.

It's a circuitous route to the large Arrow shirt factory. The plant is a real beauty, classic in design, built as a shirt factory over a century ago. The outlet is a rarity —

Kitchener

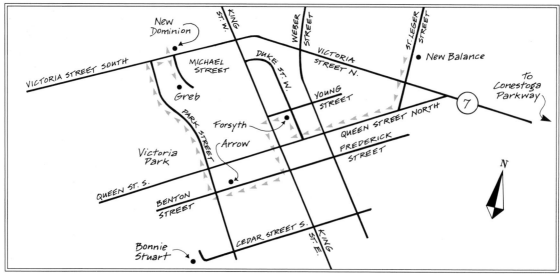

bright, spacious, tidy, with plenty of friendly staff to help. There is a broad selection of fit and colour in men's shirts, uniforms, ties, socks and pj's. Ladies' blouses and lingerie are also sold. Savings are around 50 percent, depending on quality and style.

If it's time for lunch, then there are two choices. Either picnic in Victoria Park or walk (or drive) a few blocks east along Queen to either the Walper Terrace Hotel or Cafe Mozart. If you drive, note that the Arrow parking lot has an exit to Queen Street. Walking is recommended, as it's only a few blocks and parking downtown on a Saturday can be maddening.

Cafe Mozart, 45 Queen South, has achieved legendary status locally as the best place for continental desserts and pastries. There are two dozen sweets here to choose from, as well as excellent coffee and other beverages. During the week, lunches are also sold. (Who needs sandwiches when you can have Black Forest cake?)

The Walper Terrace Hotel and its predecessors have been the popular choice among travelling businessmen, celebrities and dignitaries since the 1820s. The best place for daytrippers to lunch is the main-floor Terrace Cafe. It is also the best place to study the former glory of the hotel — tile floors, stained-glass windows, marble pillars, deep window bays — and consider what it would have been like when it was the only respectable hotel in town.

Head back to the car at Arrow. If you need to shop for children's footwear, then follow the map to Bonnie Stuart; it is a pleasant walk through a quiet, older working-class neighbourhood. Bonnie Stuart is a tiny outlet with a limited selection of shoes, runners, sandals and boots for kids. The best choices are in off-season lines. For example, load up on boots in the summer months at about 50 percent of the retail price.

Otherwise, drive north to the Greb and Cline Shirt outlets on Michael Street. This is no longer a shoe factory, although old-timers can remember when it was. The Cline factory is right upstairs. Returning university students head here each fall to purchase a new pair of Greb work boots, but this is also the place to buy Hush Puppies, golf shoes, Bauer products, dress shoes, and kids' boots and shoes. A small selection of imperfect men's dress and casual shirts in a good variety of sizes are available at the rear of the store. The best part is the delightfully friendly and helpful staff.

As you return to Victoria, look for New Dominion Bakery on the opposite side of the street. There are breads and buns sold here at discounted prices, although there is a limited variety. Pick up something to munch on while driving home.

New Balance Factory Outlet
Monday-Saturday 9:00-5:00
(519) 576-7520 ext. 20

John Forsyth Company
Tuesday-Thursday 10:00-4:00
Friday 10:00-6:00
Saturday 8:30-2:00
(519) 743-0099

The Arrow Company
Monday-Saturday 9:00-5:00
Friday 9:00-9:00
(519) 743-8211

Bonnie Stuart Shoes
Saturday 9:00-2:00
(519) 578-8880

Greb Factory Outlet
Monday-Wednesday 9:00-5:00
Thursday & Friday 9:00-9:00
Saturday 9:00-5:00
(519) 578-3500

New Dominion Bakery
Monday-Friday 8:00-6:00
Saturday & Sunday 8:00-3:00
(519) 745-8995

32 WATERLOO
A Fistful of Museums

Waterloo is one of Ontario's fastest-growing municipalities, much of this growth attributed to the presence of two universities, Wilfrid Laurier and the University of Waterloo. The University of Waterloo is now the home of five small museums which taken together are a good daytrip. This trip will also makes a stop at the Seagram Museum; the distillery is one of the area's oldest and largest employers.

The University of Waterloo is on University Avenue, in the northwest corner of the city. Public parking is across University Avenue from the entrance. Stop at the front kiosk for a campus map, an essential item in the search for campus museums.

Closest to the front of campus is the Arts Centre Gallery, in the Modern Languages building. Exhibits in this art gallery are constantly changing and range from touring exhibitions by artists of national or international repute to exhibits by fine arts students. Although the exhibitions are most often of paintings, there may be sculpture, photography or fabric works, depending on the show. The gallery space is small, built around a large theatre, but the semi-circular form means that a large number of works can be shown.

Next stop is the Biology 1 building; check those campus maps! On the third floor, a large classroom has been transformed into the Biology and Earth Sciences Museum. This museum has a diverse range of displays, from fossils to tree rings, and is a good place to show children a wide range of scientific pursuits. It would be of greatest interest to rockhounds, due to its excellent collection of minerals and crystals. There are microscopes to study crystals close up, and several computer programs to teach and test you on topics such as groundwater and volcanoes. Just to the north of the Biology building is a garden featuring many examples of rocks and minerals from across Ontario.

On to the Museum and Archive of Games, located in B.C. Matthews Hall. This may look like a small museum, but it's packed with information--and fun. The museum introduces us to a world of games through changing exhibits of games and puzzles from around the world and through the ages. Recent examples include puzzles and puzzle-making, pinball machines, and games brought to Canada by various immigrant groups. The displays are the actual game boards and pieces, set up with instructions on play. Several hours could be spent trying them all.

If you are not a real walker, it may be a good time to return to your car, drive it around to the north end of campus and park again. Across Columbia Street is the School of Optometry, and on the third floor, the Museum of Visual Sciences and Optometry. Displays trace the development of lens-making and optometry, with a multitude of glasses, lenses and contact lenses. Antique eye-examination equipment, microscopes, and optometrists' office furnishings are also featured.

Drive to the Brubacher House, on the north side of Columbia Street, overlooking Columbia Lake. This farmhouse was built in 1850 and depicts the typical life on a German Mennonite farm between 1850 and 1890. Each visitor is given a personal tour and there are also slide shows on area history and various farm and domestic skills. The guides are knowledgeable and hospitable, and without them you would miss appreciating the many unique items collected from local Mennonite families. Home design included many practical elements: a dry sink and roller-towel inside the back door, a couch for recuperating family members in the kitchen, and sturdy kitchen implements built to last a lifetime.

It's now time for dinner. After spending an afternoon on campus, you may want to eat as students do, at Angie's Kitchen, 47 Erb

Street West. The fish and chips are superb. The other choice for eating is Spirits Restaurant at the Seagram Museum. You can dine in the atmosphere of the original barrel warehouse, which has been creatively recycled as restaurant, gift shop and museum. The Seagram Museum is open late enough that you can manage an after-dinner visit.

From the moment you see the old blue shutters and the barrels in the Seagram courtyard, you know that you're entering the heart of a nineteenth-century industrial complex, and a very picturesque one at that. The spacious museum retains the feel of an old-time distillery through the generous use of original timbers and barrels.

The museum exhibits illustrate the intricacies of producing fine spirits and wine, from grain or grape to bottled product. There are also exhibits relating to the development of the Canadian distilling industry. The artifacts and displays are excellent, as are the 12 film galleries throughout the museum. There are always helpful guides to answer questions and free guided tours on Sundays at 2:00PM. Some of the most interesting equipment displays include antique glass decanters, an onion-shaped copper Scotch still, and bottling machines. There are also good exhibits dealing with the manufacture of cork, white oak barrels, and 50 years of "Drink in Moderation" advertisements.

Because all the sites included in this daytrip feature changing exhibits, museum-hopping in Waterloo can be enjoyed again and again.

Waterloo

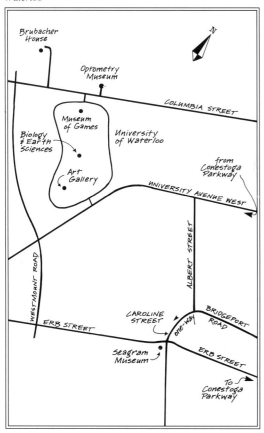

Arts Centre Gallery
Monday-Friday 11:00-4:00
Sundays 2:00-5:00 during winter
(519) 885-1211 ext. 2439

Biology and Earth Sciences Museum
Monday-Friday 9:00-5:00
(519) 885-1211 ext. 2469

Museum and Archive of Games
Monday-Friday 9:00-5:00
(519) 888-4424

Museum of Visual Science
and Optometry
Monday-Friday 8:30-4:30
(519) 885-1211 ext. 3405

Brubacher House
May-November:
Wednesday-Saturday 2:00-5:00
(519) 886-3855

Seagram Museum
Tuesday-Friday 11:00-8:00
Saturday, Sunday & Holidays
12:00-5:00
(519) 885-1857

33   ST. JACOBS
To Market, To Market

Farms without electricity, fields worked by horsepower, No Sunday Sale signs — these alert travellers to the fact that they are in a special part of the world: Mennonite Ontario. Waterloo County is the Ontario home of old-order Mennonites who live a farm life not greatly changed from that of past generations. The first German-speaking Mennonite settlers arrived in this area from Pennsylvania at the beginning of the last century, and through hard work and community solidarity, built a reputation for success in agriculture and business, and worldwide charitable works.

Appropriately, the day begins at two farm markets between the city of Waterloo and the village of St. Jacobs. Take Highway 86 (Conestoga Parkway) around the city of Waterloo to King Street North, and hence to the intersection of King and Weber streets. You can't miss the Waterloo Farmers' Market and Stockyards Market on the left (parking is off Weber Street). Plan to attend either market early in the day to avoid crowds and to partake of Oktoberfest sausage-on-a-bun, a breakfast that lasts all morning.

The Waterloo Farmers' Market began when vendors, unhappy with plans for the modernization of the Kitchener Market, moved their business to this site. The older portions of the market — the outside stalls and the building nearest Weber Street — retain a unique Mennonite character. This market is one of the best places to buy "whole foods" of every variety. It is not hard to find homemade dairy products, free-range chicken eggs, additive-free baked goods and preserves, and drug-free meat. Keep an eye out for especially indigenous wares such as maple syrup, apple butter, elderberry and shoe-fly pies, and sausage in a multitude of sizes and aromas.

The Stockyard Market, across Weber Street, is Ontario's largest farm outlet, with over 200 vendors. This is also the site of the

Ontario Livestock Exchange, the largest auction sale being on Thursday mornings, and an additional horse auction being held on Tuesdays. Children enjoy watching the auction of cattle, swine, horses and small animals, and surveying the holding pens area from the catwalk. The Stockyard includes a large flea market, so if you fancy browsing for buttons, small animals, housewares, clothing, workshop tools, and the like, this is the place to be.

The second part of this daytrip takes place in St. Jacobs (originally Jacobstettel), three kilometres north of the markets on King Street (Highway 8). It is common to see horse and plough working the fields on both sides of the highway here, and in the spring the sky is streaked with smoke rising from sugar shacks as maple syrup season progresses.

On the main street of St. Jacobs, on the right-hand side, is The Meeting Place, our next stop. This is the spot to learn about the people who give Waterloo County its distinctive appeal. The story of the Mennonite faith and unworldly way of life is told through film, slides, recordings and museum displays. The story is an inspirational one, and the museum is of high quality, so plan to include The Meeting Place in your day.

St. Jacobs is one of Ontario's best shopping villages. Folk and fine art, clothing, antiques and collectibles are housed in the refurbished Snider Flour Mill and attached silos. Ice cream is sold in a caboose and the O.J.Smith Shoe factory on Spring Street has been turned into a maple syrup museum and bookshop. A new riverside development specializes in children's books, toys and clothes.

You can spend a lot of time observing the proceedings behind the counter at the Village Bakery. With an unhurried motion, Mennonite women can peel and core an apple

THE KISSING BRIDGE AT WEST MONTROSE

For those who want to further explore Waterloo's Mennonite country before heading home, a short side trip can be taken from St. Jacobs to see Ontario's sole remaining covered bridge. This 60-metre bridge spans the Grand River in a picturesque setting at West Montrose, a town founded by Mennonite settlers in the early 1800s. The bridge is built of oak and pine and was constructed in 1881. It is called the Kissing Bridge because it affords a brief moment of privacy for courting couples passing through it — a cherished commodity in any era.

It makes a very pleasant Sunday afternoon to picnic and wander along the river park near the bridge, catching glimpses of Mennonite families riding in their buggies on the way home from their meeting houses.

---

in the time it takes to say it. Picnic supplies can be purchased here, and there are tables at the west end of the Snider Mill parking lot. If picnicking isn't for you, there are three restaurants in town. The Stone Crock serves local food family-style, Benjamin's is a newly-renovated inn, and the Mill Race Cafe is in the mill.

St. Jacobs is a good town to stroll through even if you are not a shopper. Follow the signs to Jacobstettel, a bed-and-breakfast at 16 Isabella Street, on the west side of town. It's an elegant building with intricate inlaid wood floors and ceilings. The neat grounds have a rose garden that is worth a visit.

During the final part of this visit to Mennonite country you can walk off your indulgences by strolling along the scenic millrace path. The race, Ontario's longest, was constructed over 120 years ago to provide power for the flour mills. It begins at the mill and ends two kilometres away at a dam on the Conestoga River, a favourite fishing spot among locals of all ages.

This is a favourite country walk: it is sheltered and quiet in all seasons; the bird-watching can be good in the woods and on the river; the race is shovelled for skating in winter; the path is accessible to strollers. The millrace walk allows a glimpse at the

"backsides" of a few typical farms, which makes it a fit end to a day that started with marvelling at the variety of quality foods and crafts that farm families sell at the market.

Waterloo Farmers' Market
All year:
Saturday 6:00-2:00
May-October:
Wednesday 7:00-2:00

Stockyard Farmers' Market
Thursday 7:00-1:00
Saturday 7:00-2:00
(519) 747-1830

The Meeting Place
November-April:
Saturday 11:00-4:30
Sunday 2:00-4:30
May-October:
Monday-Friday 11:00-5:00
Saturday 10:00-5:00
Sunday 1:30-5:00
(519) 664-3518

34 ELORA
Gorgeous Ontario

The pastoral countryside of the Grand River Valley north of Guelph has the modest charm common to much of rural Ontario — well-tended farms, rolling terrain, lowing cattle, the scent of hay. You would assume that there are few scenic wonders here. But, as always, travel dispels stereotypes. A dark band of evergreen forest just southeast of the village of Elora conceals a remarkable piece of Ontario.

The chasm of the Grand River is probably the most dramatic scenery in southern Ontario with the exception of Niagara Falls. Cedar forest, caves, limestone cliffs, and rapids combine to create a scene of striking beauty. And there's nearby Elora, one of the first villages refurbished for the recreational shopper.

The Elora Gorge is best explored by using the facilities of the Grand River Conservation Authority, which manages a 145-hectare park. The entrance to Elora Gorge Park is on County Road 21, which is in turn reached via Highway 6 from Guelph.

Head for the walking trail along the south side of the river for the best opportunity to study the walls of the Gorge. Averaging 25 metres in height, the pale grey cliffs are contrasted by the lively green of cedar trees that eke life out of the bare rock. Botanists love to study the Gorge walls, which are habitat for several rare ferns. Paths lead down to the riverbank and a forest of tall cedar and pine.

A landmark. to hikers, Hole-in-the-Rock is one of several caves formed by the dissolving action of water on limestone. The curving, mossy staircase through the Hole is right out of Mark Twain; Tom Sawyer is certainly lurking around the next turn.

The Elora Gorge Conservation Area is a daytrip for all seasons, although the park can become overcrowded on summer weekends.

There's stocked trout fishing, swimming in a man-made pond and the river, rafting and inner-tube paddling, and hiking on trails that remain cool on the hottest of days. There are also the usual picnicking and camping sites, and sports facilities.

During the winter the Conservation Authority maintains over nine kilometres of ski trails suited to beginning and intermediate skiers. Take care to avoid the treacherously icy cliff edges. Ski and snowshoe rentals are available at low cost, and there is a food concession (weekends only), a warming hut and washrooms. The Gorge has ice-skating and is one of the few parks around with winter camping.

It's quite possible to walk from the conservation area right into the village of Elora, but it is more convenient to drive to town and find a parking spot — no mean feat on weekends.

The hub of trendy shopping in Elora is Mill Street, in a quaint group of pre-Confederation buildings that cling to the edge of the Grand River. Each year brings more artisans and boutiques to Elora; they're now located in a mews on the north side of Mill Street, and all along Metcalfe Street. Don't be so intent on shopping that you miss appreciating the stonemasons' skill that gave picturesque form to local limestone.

There are so many shops in Elora that it is impossible to describe them all. But there are a few stores that should be mentioned simply because they offer items not easily found elsewhere. Cobwebs on Mill Street sells antique and contemporary kitchenwares. Whether you're interested in a terra-cotta onion-keeper ("ideal for use at home or on safari"), herb-drying hooks, or butter and biscuit moulds, this is the place for you. Adderfox Antiques on Metcalfe sells original and reproduction Canadian primitive furnishings. The furniture is a change from the

Riverview, Elora

typical antique store offerings — durable and practical, finished in authentic pioneer shades.

The casual cotton clothing from Ecuador sold at the Magic Mountain Trading Company comes in a range of breathtaking colours. Reason enough to visit the shop on the boardwalk hidden behind the Mill Street stores. Another reason is that this is a great spot to sit and enjoy the sunlight glinting off the water and the sound of the falls. Don't miss it in winter, when there's not a soul in sight and the sun warms your stone backrest to a toasty temperature.

No day of hiking, skiing or shopping could be complete without a good meal, and Elora has restaurants to suit every budget. The most noteworthy is The Elora Mill Inn and Restaurant, Ontario's sole surviving five-storey mill. The view of the Gorge is spectacular, the food first-rate. Fine dining and accommodation are also available at the Metcalfe Inn. The Desert Rose Cafe on Mill Street has an international vegetarian menu; wholesome and delicious food at terrific prices. It also offers bed-and-breakfast accommodation. The Great Escape Tea Room offers an unconventional combination of lunches and sweets.

A day in Elora will remind you how wonderful it is to live in gorgeous Ontario.

Elora Gorge Conservation Area
mid-October to late April:
9:00-4:30
May to mid-October:
Daily to dusk
(519) 846-9742

Most shops and restaurants
open daily

35 FERGUS
The Scottish Connection

The Scottish element in the character of Ontario is as thick as porridge and about as enduring. Scots were among our first pioneers, and with their numerous descendants, they left an indelible mark on the landscape. Beautifully crafted stone buildings, scores of place names, highland games and dances — these are all common Scottish elements found in Ontario to this day. One of the best places to appreciate our Scottish heritage is in Fergus, the Grand River mill town north of Guelph.

Town founders Adam Fergusson and James Webster purchased land around the Grand River in Nichol Township and sold parcels to specially selected friends and relatives from Scotland. Initially a mill town, Fergus later became home to foundries and machine shops. The town has a remarkable heritage of nineteenth-century buildings bearing the mark of skilled Scots stonemasons.

Head for the Fergus Market, located on the south bank of the Grand River at St. David Street (Highway 6). Plan to leave the car here awhile. The building dates to 1877, when it was built as a foundry. On Saturdays and Sundays it is abustle with visitors and regulars buying cheese, meat, vegetables, crafts and home baking. It's half farm market and half craft fair. There are several places in the market to purchase lunch, and it can be eaten on a pleasant little patio overlooking the Grand River. The market building also houses the Chamber of Commerce, where you can pick up a historical walking tour brochure.

The Scottish element in Fergus is evident at the Hearth and Heather shop on the second floor of the market. Here you'll find British foods such as lemon barley water, plum pudding, and beer shandy. There are kilts, ties and everything else in tartans. There are also over 1,000 titles on subjects dear to Highlanders, such as Celtic legends, clan ancestries and Scottish history.

If you are eager for more of the Scottish connection, Fergus hosts North America's largest highland games the first weekend in August each year, with bands, dancers and athletes.

Across the river from the market is the old livery building (1878) housing a cheese deli which sells Woolwich Dairy's fine goat cheese. There are also craft shops and a restaurant. One of the town's early inhabitants was Abraham Groves, builder of Ontario's first electric light plant, across St. David from the livery. It is now called Groves Mill and is a House of Brougham furniture store.

Continue your Fergus tour by walking west on St. Andrew. Most of this streetscape

Fergus Market

dates to the mid-1800s, and it is remarkably complete. Some of the buildings are faced with reddish sandstone, while others have been left natural grey limestone. Don't miss number 245, which has an intact first-floor facade (rather unusual in Ontario downtowns) and decorative woodwork around the eaves.

On the south side of St. Andrew is an alley leading to secluded Templin Gardens on the Grand River. This is a quiet bit of lawn and perennial flower beds, perfect for a picnic lunch.

Continue along St. Andrew to Breadalbane, and the stone Breadalbane Inn. It offers accommodations and meals; lunch and dinner during the week, and dinner on weekends. The interesting menu, with everything from seafood to glazed ribs, is given an A+ by most reviewers.

Turn away from the river on Breadalbane, walk to St. Patrick and turn east. Fergus has over 160 stone homes, and many of them are located in these blocks. These historic homes have signs noting not only the date of their construction, but also the occupation of the original owner. We can get a good introduction to early Ontario by locating the residences of blacksmiths, merchants, doctors, and so on. No Scots town would be complete without a Presbyterian Church, and the one in Fergus has a commanding position above the town at Tower Street and St. George. Continue along St. Patrick to St. David Street and return to the car at the market.

Fergus has many side streets worth exploring, but one of the nicest is Union Street, just south of the market. This is a picturesque neighbourhood of solid stone and gingerbread mansions set on broad lawns.

No trip to Grand River country is complete without a swim at the quarry on the north side of the river between Fergus and Elora. Drive west on St. Andrew to reach the Elora Quarry Conservation Area.

The quarry is best early in the day, when the sun glints off the emerald water, reflect-ing the limestone cliffs with the cedar fringe on top. There's a beach area with shallow entry to the water, suitable for children (only life jackets allowed, no water wings), and a deep, cool quarry for everyone else. There are also picnic spots and hiking trails.

This has been a taste of Scottish Ontario, from limestone cottages to tartan kilts. And nowhere more picturesque than at Fergus.

Fergus Market
Saturday 8:00-5:00
Sunday 9:00-5:00
(519) 843-5221

Elora Quarry
May-October:
Daily 10:00-8:00
(519) 846-9742

36 GUELPH
Galleria Guelph

There are several good reasons to spend a daytrip in Guelph. It has an attractive university campus, a fine stone downtown, a Spring Festival for the arts, and miles of riverside parkland. But for the connoisseur of fine art and crafts, there is a rich assortment of studios and galleries located within convenient walking distances of one another. (Note that most are closed Sunday.)

The first stop of the day is at the at the Macdonald Stewart Art Centre, on the University of Guelph campus. A historic red-brick building houses over 3,000 Canadian works. The building itself is a work of art: the recent additions, cleverly designed by architect Raymond Moriyama, blend inconspicuously with the original dignity of the building. The centre includes a spacious outdoor sculpture garden.

A special feature of the centre, and one not to be missed, is the Omark collection of Inuit art — collages, drawings, prints and carvings. Study Canadian geography by locating the home of the artists on the map provided, and study Arctic zoology by scrutinizing the various bones and antlers used for carving.

The Barber Gallery on Suffolk Street, the upper floor of an old warehouse, houses fine art in paint, glass, clay, stone, fabric, and just about ever other media going. There are original works by artists of local, national and international repute, as well as those whose reputation is not yet made. It is a great place to drink in beauty for its own sake, as well as to purchase some for "take-out."

After locating a parking spot in the central part of Guelph, the rest of the day can be spent on foot. Convenient parking is found throughout the downtown, and one can choose a location according to how much or how little one wants to walk.

The first studio of the day is Designer Glass. While this spot is an inspiration to anyone interested in brightening an interior, it can be an especially rewarding visit for those renovating an older home. This is the place to find out how stained-glass overlays and etched glass can be used to turn ordinary doors, cabinets, windows and room dividers into pieces of functional art.

The most appropriate lunch spot for a studio tour in Guelph is The Bookshelf, and some residents of the Royal City think it's the only place to recommend to visitors. The menu is international, the staff infectiously friendly, and the walls display the work of local artists. A different artist is featured each month or so, and for the interested patron, a brief biography is usually hanging in the reception area of the cafe.

The ample portions served at The Bookshelf will have you ready to do some more wandering, so head for Vessels on Wyndham Street. Goldie Sherman's studio reflects the vibrancy of the artist. The shelves are crammed with pottery glazed in brilliant blues and greens that are a welcome shock after the dreary stairway one climbs to reach the studio. But the climb is worth it. There are so many unique creations here: mugs with whimsical creatures hidden at the bottom, apple bakers, oil lamps, ingenious butter dishes that keep butter both soft and fresh, honey pots, and salt cellars. Charming inlaid wood boxes by David Atkinson are also sold here.

A dramatic change of pace awaits at Walter Zimochod Jewellers — quiet opulence, not exactly for the casual browser, but then this isn't an ordinary studio. You can watch a master jeweller painstakingly create delicate custom works in gold and silver: necklaces, pendants, charms, earrings, brooches. Stone pieces and gems are also on display.

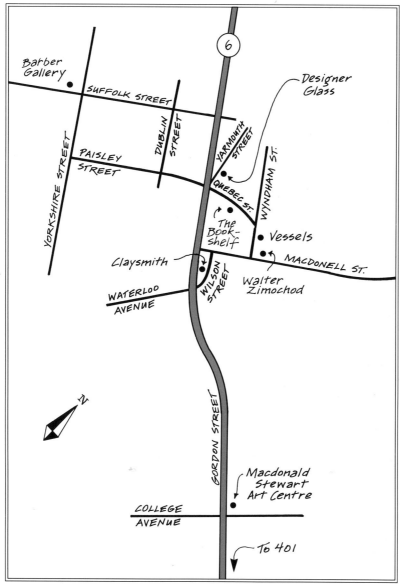

Guelph

Claysmith on Wilson Street is the last visit of the day. There's a good variety of pottery here, from decorative works to very practical ones such as batter bowls and baking dishes. Here, too, are glass and ceramic sculpture, and jewellery. Valerie Hoggs has a selection of clothing at Claysmith, including nostalgic and contemporary uses of tie-dyed fabrics.

By this point in the day it's time to return home, unpack your purchases, and decide exactly where to hang that new picture or properly display the latest in sculpture.

Macdonald Stewart Art Centre
Tuesday-Sunday 12:00-5:00
(519) 837-0010

Most studios closed
Sunday and Monday

37 ROCKWOOD
History in Motion

"All aboard," cried the blue-suited conductor, and he followed us up the stairs into the electric street-railway car marked "Bloor-Parliament." Punching our tickets, he remarked that it was too warm to light the coal furnace at the back door of the trolley. The quiet rock of the trolley made a soothing accompaniment for surveying the surrounding woodlot, where trilliums heralded the arrival of spring.

A dream? Yes, and no. Yes, it was the dream of Sir Adam Beck, the founder of Ontario Hydro, that southern Ontario be connected by electric railways radiating from each major city. No, it is reality, for Beck's dream is alive and in motion at the Halton Country Radial Railway. The HCRR is located on the Guelph Line, 16 kilometres north of the 401.

This museum is dedicated to rescuing and restoring electric railway cars. Each car is a piece of Ontario history, and many would have been scrap if it were not for the efforts of the museum. These efforts have been so successful that 16 years after its official public opening, the museum includes over three dozen electric railcars and work vehicles, a mile of track, restoration and storage garages, and the Rockwood railway station.

It is most pleasant to ride any of these railcars on the 20-minute round trip through the woodlot. You can disembark at the end loop and examine electric snowsweepers and track grinders before returning to the starting-point on a later car.

Car 327 is especially suited to fair-weather visits. This small, open-sided car was built by the Toronto Transit Commission in 1933 following plans for streetcars of 1893. The quaint charm of Number 327 includes the following details: decorative woodwork on the seats, fish-net fenders known as pedestrian-pushers, and brightly-striped awnings which would keep centre seats dry during showers. The 327s had their running boards removed when they proved hazardous to the ever-increasing automobile traffic sharing the streets.

The most fascinating part of the Halton County Radial Railway is the restoration garage. From the intricacies of mechanical and electrical parts to interior decoration, these vehicles are being restored to an authentic condition. Volunteers, some coming from great distances, work patiently from original shop drawings and specifications.

Perhaps the most interesting piece of restoration is that of Car 8. Number 8 was built by the Jewett Car Company (Newark, Ohio) in 1915 as a prototype for Beck's interurban transit scheme. The scheme failed, and most of the Number 8s were sold for scrap.

This massive beauty (47 1/2 tons) would have zipped along the London-Port Stanley line at 100 kilometres an hour, carrying partyers to the dance hall on Lake Erie. It is easy to imagine travellers dressed in their finery against the backdrop of stained-glass windows and gleaming woodwork.

One can also visit the relocated Rockwood station, which is under restoration, and see the ticket office, photographs of rail years gone by, and the switchboard. There are picnicking spots at the museum, as well as a snack bar and gift shop.

When you tire of riding the rails at the Halton County Radial Railway, a refreshing change of pace awaits at the Rockwood Conservation Area. It's certainly easy to find: drive five kilometres north on Guelph Line to Highway 7, turn east (right), and almost immediately the Conservation Area sign indicates another right turn.

The park has two main focuses of activity, each with different character and facilities.

Number 327

The western end has a heavily used beach, concession, shelter and sports field. The quieter, eastern portion of the park (sadly lacking a washroom) is recommended because it provides a better opportunity to relax without dodging Frisbees. You can picnic amidst the picturesque ruins of the Harris Woolen Mill, enjoying the babbling of the minnow-filled stream.

Two large millponds are used for paddle-boating and canoeing. Rentals are at western millpond; wisely, no motorboats are permitted. Smallmouth bass, northern pike and rainbow trout apparently inhabit the waters, and even lack of success in fishing for them hasn't dimmed Rockwood's appeal.

The hiking in Rockwood is good, considering its limited size (80 hectares) and proximity to urbanized areas. Trails run to scenic lookouts over both sides of the Eramosa River. At the eastern end of the park, a paved road (no auto access) takes you to an uncrowded area overlooking the upper end of the millpond. It is easy to forget the hustle and bustle as you watch kingfishers dive or explore Rockwood's caves.

Another interesting walk connects the two ends of the park along the north side of the larger millpond. The irregular limestone topography is radically different from that of the surrounding farmland. Footbridges cross deep, perfectly round pools called "potholes." The most prevalent theory regarding their origin is that they were ground out of the soft limestone by boulders carried by swirling glacial meltwaters.

From electric power to foot power, this busy trip will have you ready to return home, via Highway 7, or the Guelph Line and the 401.

Halton County Radial Railway
June:
Wednesday-Sunday 10:00-5:00
July & August:
Daily 10:00-5:00
May, September, October:
Saturday, Sunday &
Holidays 10:00-5:00
(519) 856-9802

Rockwood Conservation Area
May-October:
Daily 8:00-dusk
(519) 621-2761

38 CAMPBELLVILLE
Birds of a Feather

Mother Nature celebrates springtime in Ontario in so many marvellous ways, making amends for what can seem to be an unnecessarily long and icy winter. The word spring evokes a variety of images, but two of the most widely cherished are the sweetness of fresh maple syrup and the calls of returning geese. Both of these may be relished to the fullest at the Mountsberg Wildlife Centre. Take Highway 6 south from the 401 and follow signs east to Mountsberg; or from Campbellville, take Regional Road 9 west and follow signs.

Visit Mountsberg on weekends and holidays from early March to mid-April. From the time of the first drip-drip-drip of melting snow, sap moves upwards in the black and sugar maple trees used to produce syrup. The warm days and freezing nights required to produce copious sap flow are a special characteristic of spring thaw in southern Ontario.

Your maple adventure commences at the Interpretive Centre, with films and slide shows on maple syrup production. From mid-morning to late afternoon, Mountsberg Percherons pull wagonloads of visitors to the Sugar Bush. Displays along a half-kilometre trail describe the history of maple syrup technology. Indians taught the first settlers how to collect and boil sap, and the tradition, somewhat modified by modern technology, has passed from generation to generation in rural families. The Sugar Bush includes a sugar house with modern evaporator, and a candy store with a maple theme.

The climax of the Mountsberg maple syrup program is the Pancake House, where visitors eat their fill of pancakes and sausage at outdoor tables, savouring the scent of wood fires and the first warm spring breezes. This is, in a sense, a re-enactment of the "sugaring off" celebrations that are older than the province.

Another herald of spring in Ontario is the migration of large waterfowl, particularly geese and swans. Southwestern Ontario is on a major flyway, or bird migration route, and most of us admit to a thrill at the sound of a large flock of Canada geese passing overhead. Mountsberg, with its 200-hectare lake, is a magnet for birds feeding and loafing en route to the Arctic. In all, about 35 species of waterfowl visit during migration and at least 7 of these species stay to nest and rear young. Many thousand may visit at a time, adding to the area's reputation as a place to watch spring unfold. There is a lakeside observation tower on the north end of the reservoir, access by Town Line Road.

Mountsberg is also well known as a place to study birds at close range. The staff specialize in rehabilitating wild birds of prey (owls, hawks, falcons, eagles); birds can be viewed in the Interpretive Centre and in outdoor pens. Resident buffalo and elk are in pens of their own nearby. Children wanting to pet an animal should head for the historic barn with its chickens, goats, horses and sheep.

Mountsberg rates a visit by an outdoor enthusiast in any season. Several kilometres of hiking and ski trails traverse a wide range of wildlife habitat — cedar and hardwood forests, swampland, streams and fields. There are trail interpretive brochures, including one for a nature trivia trail. A ski and snowshoe rental shop operates when weather permits. And you may want to come in the fall to see the southbound bird migration.

Our spring trip continues to the northwest, at the Kortright Waterfowl Park. Follow County Road 9 west to Highway 6, and hence north to the 401; take the 401 west to the Hanlon Expressway (Highway 6 north). Kortright Road is a major intersection on the expressway, and our destination lies two kilometres west.

Mallard, Kortright

Forty-seven hectares, largely cedar wetland and stream, have been developed as a waterfowl propagation and rehabilitation centre. Over 90 species of ducks, geese and swans from around the world form the captive population. Wild birds, attracted by the choice habitat and by their caged brethren, swell the numbers of waterfowl to the hundreds. This is probably the easiest way to get a good look at the retiring wood duck, or to see nesting Canada geese at arm's length. All races of Canada geese may be seen, from the diminutive Richardson's race to the magnificent Atlantic race. A springtime visit to Kortright is very rewarding, for waterfowl nest very early, and one is sure to spot downy young taking their first swimming lessons or riding on their parents' backs.

There are several gravelled hiking trails in the sanctuary. Kortright deer are notoriously bold and are usually spotted on the trails a dozen yards from busy Kortright Road.

Kortright includes a picnic area, playground, amphitheatre and a visitor centre. If picnicking is not in your plans, return to the Hanlon Expressway, head south to the Aberfoyle Road, and turn east. Upon entering Aberfoyle, turn south, and at the south end of town find the Aberfoyle Mill restaurant.

The Aberfoyle Mill is correctly identified as the spot to sample "fine dining in the country." There are several large dining rooms, each decorated with old farm implements and antiques befitting a building of approximately 130 years. You can dine to the tinkle of either a piano or the millstream, or both, depending on your location. The food receives rave reviews from customers, as does the polished service. Prices are moderate at dinner, and a steal at lunch.

Fill your lungs with a last breath of spring air, gather your flock about you, and fly for home.

Kortright Waterfowl Park
Daily, year-round: 10:00-5:00
(519) 824-6729

Mountsberg Wildlife Centre
Daily, year-round: 9:00-5:00
(416) 854-2276

Aberfoyle Old Mill Restaurant
Daily, year-round: 11:30-9:00
(519) 763-1070

39 ANCASTER
A Taste of the Past

Most Ontarians live in large cities. We don't often think about what Ontario might have looked like before settlement, and we are unfamiliar with the progression from forest to farm to mill to town. How fortunate that a daytrip within one of our most highly urbanized areas can provide an overview of this metamorphosis.

Begin at the Dundas Valley Conservation Area, on Governor's Road (Road 399) just north of Ancaster, on Hamilton's fringe. Dundas Valley is embraced on two sides by the Niagara Escarpment, and the terrain is rugged — steep hills, unlogged forest, cascading brooks. The majesty of the forest, the quality of the hiking trails, the serenity of the valley, are unparalleled in southern Ontario.

There's much here for the ardent naturalist. These woods are the habitat for plants and animals typically found much farther south, in the Carolinian forest; hence this is a prime place to see flowering dogwood, sassafras, the Louisiana waterthrush, the golden-winged warbler, and other southerners. Because the Conservation Area comprises many different types of landscape (field, orchards, wet and dry forest), it is possible to study the transition from one habitat type to another as the area reverts from man-managed to native forest.

There are a variety of ways to experience Dundas Valley. Possibilities include skiing (36 kilometres for intermediate and advanced skiers, warming huts, snack bar, ski rentals on weekends only), snowshoeing, tobogganing, ice-skating, fitness circuits and hiking. There's a busy schedule of special events, from bird-house building to sleigh rides. Find out about all of these at the Trail Centre on Governor's Road.

The Trail Centre is also an educational place. First-rate interpretive displays highlight the complex relationships between man and nature in the Dundas vicinity. Photographs and text illustrate the succession of human settlement from remote farms in tiny forest clearings, through mills and railways (the centre is a recreated Victorian train station used in the filming of *Anne of Green Gables*), to modern mechanized farms and cities.

It's time to taste some of that marvellous history first-hand. Leave the Trail Centre, take Governor's Road west to Sulphur Springs Road and turn south. Country sideroad driving is superb: packed dirt and gravel, steep hills, precipitous curves. Upon arrival in Ancaster, drive east to the intersection of Mohawk Road and Highway 2, and signs for the Ancaster Old Mill. The Mill is actually on Old Dundas Road, entered from further east.

Dundas Valley Conservation Area

The Ancaster Old Mill appears to grow right out of the rockface of the Escarpment. It certainly may have put down roots: it was built in 1792, making it ancient by Ontario standards. The original mill building is open for tours only by advance request. It is enough to eat in the restaurant located beside the original mill, perched on the edge of the millstream; the rushing water mesmerizes and total relaxation takes over. And at last, an eatery in a restored mill that serves authentic old-Ontario food. Popular dishes include old-fashioned chicken pot pie, and pork with homemade applesauce. The emphasis is on freshly prepared foods with no additives. The original miller's house is now a bakery and gift shop, selling mill-ground flour, as well as homemade goodies.

The rest of the day can be spent exploring Ancaster, the quiet historic town that grew up around the Mill. (Note how many streets are named for mill owners — a list of owners is on the Mill menu.) There are several possibilities for exploring, depending on whether you visit during the week or on a Sunday.

Wednesday through Saturday travellers may want to stop in at Kershaw's Old Maps and Prints at 442 Wilson Street (Ancaster's main street). This stop is a dream come true for those with a penchant for maps and antique prints covering subjects from natural history to Canadian history. Some prints date to the sixteenth century. Relevant to today's daytrip is the collection of maps and prints illustrating life over two centuries in the Ancaster and Hamilton area.

Bennett's Apples & Cider has been an integral part of Ancaster since 1911, when Charlie Bennett and family purchased the farm. In 1917 a roadside cider mill began operation, a service popular with neighbourhood children. On weekdays you can watch the cider mill in operation. The store sells not only apples, but also famous cider doughnuts, cider vinegar and fresh local honey. Add a mill for fresh-ground peanut butter, fresh vegetables, and you have a farm superstore. And to think that it's been happening here for almost 80 years. Bennett's

is on Highway 53 south of Ancaster, just east of Southcote Road.

For those daytripping on Sunday, when Kershaw's and Bennett's are closed, a good alternative is Fieldcote, Ancaster's brand-new cultural centre. The estate home and seven picturesque acres are located on Sulphur Springs Road. Changing gallery displays focus on local themes, contemporary or historical. There's a good collection of historical photographs that provide incentive for further exploration in town. (Fieldcote closes for exhibit changes, so phone ahead to check on hours.)

Daytripping in Ancaster leaves us well-excercised, well-fed, and a little more alert to the processes shaping Ontario's landscape.

Dundas Valley Conservation Area
Daily, year-round:
9:00-dusk
Trail Centre, weekends only
(416) 627-1233

Fieldcote Memorial Park & Museum
Wednesday, Thursday, Friday, Sunday
1:00-5:00
(416) 648-8144

Ancaster Old Mill Inn
Daily, year-round:
11:30-9:00
Sunday Brunch 10:00-2:00
(416) 648-1827

Kershaw's Old Maps and Prints
Wednesday-Saturday 10:00-5:00
(416) 648-1991

Bennett's Apples & Cider
Monday-Thursday &
Saturday 9:00-6:00
Friday 9:00-9:00
(416) 648-6878

40 DUNDAS
Spring Thaw

There's nothing quite as sweet as an Ontario spring. Cerulean skies, witch hazel and crocus, brimming streams, fresh breezes. One of the best places to start savouring springtime is in downtown Dundas. Dundas? Yes, a country spring can be had right in the centre of the Golden Horseshoe.

Spring starts early in Dundas: the land slopes south to catch the sun, and temperatures are moderated by Lake Ontario. At the Ben Veldhuis Greenhouse complex, there are signs of spring in early March, before school break heralds official spring, and long before there's any significant action in the home garden. Ben Veldhuis is on King Street East, the main street of Dundas, at the very eastern edge of town.

Primula, narcissus and tulips offer a perfumed welcome; it's impossible to pass by without taking another grateful inhalation. The complex comprises over 20 greenhouses — acres of camellia, orchids, philodendrons and palms. Consult the directory behind the cash desk to locate your favourite. Or just meander, luxuriating in the warm sunlight and moist air.

Ben Veldhuis is known as the Cactus Capital of Canada, and deservedly so, for there are over 400 fascinating varieties here, from colourful dwarfs in five-centimetre pots to cactus vines over 10 metres long. For those who long for the Old West, save your travel dollar and linger in the giant cacti display, giving a wide berth to the thorns, spines and barbs. These are houseplants to be treated with respect — at least the cat will never eat them!

Take a last look at spring under glass before heading out of doors for the remainder of the day. Before getting in the car, you may like to feed the geese in the old canal beside the greenhouses. Head west, through downtown Dundas, stopping at a deli to pick up the fixings for the first picnic of the year. For ready-made sandwiches, there's the Espresso Cafe; homemade corned beef, and baklava, at its sweet and sticky best, are neighbourhood favourites.

King Street turns into Highway 8; follow this west, zigzagging up the Niagara Escarpment. Don't miss the view of pretty Dundas on the way up. As the highway curves

Dundas

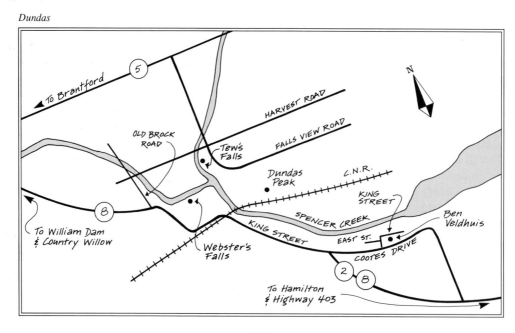

94

The Cactus Capital of Canada

sharply left, stay to the right and head off on Old Brock Road. Turn right at the intersection with Harvest Road and follow the signs to Spencer Gorge Wilderness Area.

The Gorge is a huge parkland and urban wilderness, well worth several hours of picnicking and exploring. There are two waterfalls, Tew's and Webster's, each equally picturesque. Tew's Falls, on a branch of Spencer Creek, are only a few metres shorter in height than those at Niagara, and are actually more photogenic then their Escarpment cousins, due to their unspoiled surroundings. The water cascades down rugged terraces in a narrow gorge, and the entire scene is framed by ferns, orchids and other moisture-lovers.

Follow the walking trail (a portion of the famous Bruce Trail) south to Webster's Falls. Originally part of a country estate, Webster's Falls are surrounded by picnicking spots and gardens. After the first mild days of spring, rain and melting snow combine to swell Spencer Creek to flood stage, and the tumult of Webster's Falls can be heard long before the falls are in view.

The hiking at Spencer Gorge is about the best in the area. Spring is heralded here in many ways: woodland wildflowers appear earlier than in much of the rest of the province, and migrating landbirds congregate in the gorge before continuing their journey. A spectacular panorama of the Escarpment and the Golden Horsehoe beyond unfolds all along the brink of the gorge. Take the trail from Tew's Falls along the eastern side of the Gorge to Dundas Peak for the best lookout points.

Our spring outing continues along Highway 8 north. About 10 kilometres north of Dundas is the Country Willow Restaurant (closed Mondays). If fine spring weather has

95

Webster's Falls

turned capricious and cancelled a picnic, then this is a good place to have lunch. The Willow was built in 1840 as a store and post office, and it served in that capacity until 1981, making it the oldest continuously operating post office in the country. The prices, especially on daily specials, are modest; the nostalgic aroma of the wood fire contributes to the homey atmosphere. Try and sit in one of the rear rooms, facing the back garden, so as to continue spring-watching.

There's nothing like a good ramble to revitalize dragging winter spirits. Why not take advantage of that energy and commence your spring planting. There's no place better to begin than at William Dam Seeds, just north of the Country Willow on Highway 8. William Dam has been a favourite of gardeners for decades. This unpretentious store is a treasure trove for green-thumbs seeking organic pest remedies, untreated seeds, and hard-to-find vegetable, flower and tree varieties. There are also soil mixes, jiffy pots and every other accessory. If it's not at William Dam's, you don't need it.

While Dundas is beautiful in spring, the fall colours at Spencer Gorge are magnificent.

Ben Veldhuis
Daily 8:00-5:00
Closed Sundays October-March
(416) 628-6307

Spencer Gorge Wilderness Area
Daily, year-round: 9:00-sundown

William Dam Seeds
Monday-Friday 9:00-6:00
Saturday 9:00-5:00
Extended hours April-July
Closed Saturday July-September
Closed Sunday & Holidays
Phone to confirm hours
(416) 628-6641

41 HAMILTON
Industrial Revolutions

During the mid-nineteenth century, Hamilton was an ordinary port town of about 10,000, advantageously situated on the western end of Lake Ontario. This adventure will touch on the contributions of two individuals who were key in the transformation of Hamilton into one of Canada's most heavily industrialized cities.

Our story begins at Dundurn, the elegant home of Allan Napier McNab, army colonel, businessman and lawyer. As a co-founder of the Great Western Railway, McNab brought rail service to Hamilton; the town became a transportation centre for goods and people travelling between the United States, Upper Canada, and inland frontiers. McNab's life as a public figure culminated in his becoming Prime Minister of Upper Canada in 1854, a position held until 1856. McNab died at Dundurn in 1862.

Dundurn was constructed for McNab in three years during the mid-1830s, and the interior is authentically restored to a style of decoration typical of the middle part of the last century. The expanse of pale stonework and tall windows must have been an impressive sight to those of the surrounding community. The home has an equally imposing setting, isolated on a cliff top with a commanding view of Burlington Bay.

Costumed guides conduct tours which provide a fascinating picture of life upstairs and downstairs in a grand and prosperous household. Despite Dundurn's genteel appearance, it may not have been a comfortable home by modern standards: monthly cold baths and drapes continually closed to keep out winter wind were two reminders that Canada was still a place for the vigorous.

Tours last about 45 minutes, but plan to spend some time exploring the grounds, with their aviary and gardens (under restoration to a style in keeping with that of the house).

Special events are held throughout the summer and holiday periods; concerts, including children's performances, are given in the theatre on the grounds.

The next segment of the daytrip is a drive along Burlington Street, a tour which passes some of Canada's best-known manufacturers: Stelco, Dofasco, Case, Westinghouse and General Electric. The immensity of these plants and the impersonal industrial landscape is a sharp contrast to the refinement of Dundurn and yet McNab's railway was instrumental to the development of this stretch of industry.

Upon reaching the end of Burlington Street, turn right onto Woodward Avenue and navigate by the tall stack of Hamilton's Museum of Steam and Technology. This is the next stop.

The focal point of the museum is Hamilton's first water-pumping station, built in 1859. City fathers decided that a clean water supply was required to prevent the epidemics of cholera and typhus which periodically swept

Dundurn Castle

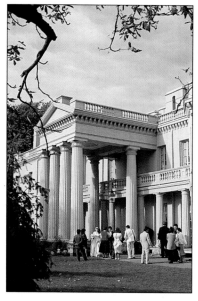

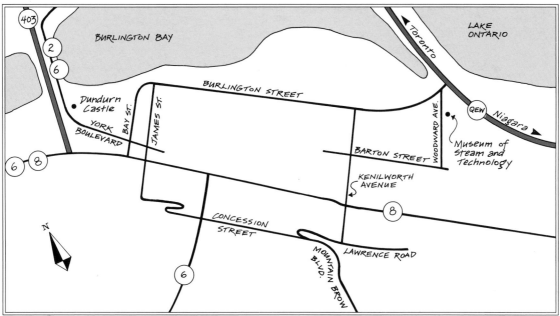

Hamilton

the city. In addition, like all cities of the last century, Hamilton was subject to fires, which spread quickly through the portside wooden buildings. A city with adequate water pressure for firefighting had an advantage in the competition for attracting industry.

Into this scene steps engineer extraordinaire Thomas Coltrin Keefer. With foresight Keefer proposed a system to draw water from Lake Ontario and not nearby Burlington Bay, thus ensuring a sufficient supply even after Hamilton's rapid growth. This waterworks was one of the highlights of a varied career and won Keefer a reputation as North America's foremost hydraulic engineer.

The pump-house is the highlight of this entire day and is a gem of Victorian industrial architecture. While the building is solid stone outside, it is gleaming brass and ornate woodwork inside. The steam-powered engines have been lovingly restored to their original operation, and one can watch the quiet revolutions of the huge flywheels, each weighing 10 tonnes and measuring over 7 metres across. The isolation of the building, its steamy atmosphere and the soft creaking of the machinery create a distinctly Dickensian atmosphere.

Thus, with Keefer's water system and McNab's railway, Hamilton emerged as an industrial giant in Central Canada. One can view the results from the top of Hamilton Mountain. Take Woodward Avenue south to Barton Street, then west (right) to Kenilworth, and follow signs or topography to Mountain Brow Boulevard. There are several parks for picnicking along Concession Street at the top of the mountain, each with spectacular views of residential Hamilton and the industrial fringe along the bay.

Dundurn Castle
June to Labour Day:
Daily 11:00-4:00
Labour Day to mid-June:
Daily 1:00-4:00
(416) 522-5313

Hamilton Museum of Steam & Technology
June to Labour Day:
Daily 11:00-4:00
Labour Day to mid-June:
Daily 1:00-4:00
(416) 549-5225

42 BURLINGTON
A Thing of Beauty is a Joy Forever

Ever had a day when you craved a fresh perspective, a little more vibrancy and colour, an out-of-the-ordinary afternoon escape? Then this daytrip is for you. It's an all-season trip, and suitable for any day of the week. The trip focuses on Burlington, which is the fortunate location of two places that help to make the world a little more beautiful: the Burlington Cultural Centre and the Royal Botanical Gardens.

First the bad news. There is no great surge of anticipation as you approach the Burlington Cultural Centre on Lakeshore Boulevard. Single-storey concrete-block buildings rarely house sources of inspiration; they look like public health clinics. Now the good news. You're in for a sweet surprise. This is a place of inspiration, beauty, serenity, humour, and new perspectives on art galleries.

There is a fresh approach to community art centres in action here, and as a result, both the building and its contents are a little out of the ordinary. Intimate and inviting, the building is a series of narrow corridors bright with displays. An open, and airy feeling results from the extensive use of natural light that comes from behind the art: each case has a window for a backdrop. This means that there is no annoying glare from artificial lighting, and that art can be studied against the backdrop of restless Lake Ontario.

Just as the Burlington Cultural Centre is not just another gallery, its greenhouse is not just another place to enjoy primula, shrimp plant and pineapple in bloom. The greenhouse is also a gallery, where all sorts of delightful ceramic creatures peek out at you from behind the greenery.

The Cultural Centre opened in 1978, and in 1983 decided to focus its permanent collection on contemporary Canadian artists working with clay. Don't groan — this is not more mug sets. This is the place where "craft" is elevated to the level of art,

communicating the ideas and individual character of the artist. The decision to remain contemporary gives the centre an upbeat air, as does the good humour expressed in many of the works. The work of the other craft guilds housed here are also on display: photography, fine arts, sculpting and wood-carving, rug-hooking, handweaving and spinning.

The centre works hard to be user-friendly: about 1,400 students a year take courses from the various guilds, from day-long to full-term sessions. And a saunter through the centre enables one to peek into the studios, where looms stand at the ready, something is baking in the kiln, and artists stand discussing the finer points of painting. This is an active place.

Burlington has a few eateries on its main drag, Brant Street, a few of blocks east of the Cultural Centre. A little farther east is Village Square, a reproduction Victorian shopping and restaurant district. For those visiting from May to October, the best place for lunch is the tea house in the rose garden at the Royal Botanical Gardens, our next stop.

To reach the Royal Botanical Gardens, follow Brant Street north to Plains Road, and head west. Although the gardens are spread out over a number of facilities, the best place to begin a tour is at the Visitor Centre on Plains Road.

At the Royal Botanical Gardens, gardening is a never-ending cycle. It can be said to begin in January, with springtime in the Mediterranean Garden greenhouse complex — a spring that lasts for six months. The intoxicating perfume of hundreds of spring bulbs introduces the Mediterranean Garden. The bulb is a protection against the heat and drought of summer, and it is interesting to see how many of our spring flowers are from Mediterranean areas.

100

Passionflower, Royal Botanical Gardens

Next comes a double-decker glass house with quiet patios, styled after those found in the gardens of southern Europe. The gardens overflow with natural and domesticated plants of those areas of the world that have hot, dry summers and mild, wet winters. It is a marvelous place to pick up ideas on plant arrangement for indoors or out. And it may be your only chance to see some exotica from the plant world; for example, the bird of paradise flower, with orange and purple blossoms resembling the decorative feathers on a bird's head, or the passionflower, used by missionaries to teach Christianity.

Outdoors activities at the Royal Botanical Gardens begin with maple syrup season in March; in April spring bulbs appear in the tens of thousands; one of the world's largest lilac gardens goes into action in late May; irises and roses of every hue initiate summer; perennials are displayed in dazzling diversity from mid-summer on; in autumn everyone looks to Mother Nature to provide the beauty; and winter brings cross-country skiing and snowshoeing.

A map, guide and advice at the Visitor Centre is a must in order to see all that the gardens have to offer. For the naturalist there are over 50 kilometres of trails and lots of wildlife, through the Arboretum, Cootes

Paradise Sanctuary (a wetland area), and the Hendrie Valley (hawthorn savannah and upland forest); for the home gardener there's lots to learn at the vegetable and herb gardens, or in the areas devoted to specimen trees, hedges and flowering shrubs; for children there are plenty of activities at their own garden centre; for botanists there is a superb bookshop, medicinal gardens and a fragrance garden.

This day has been devoted to beauty, from handcrafted clayworks to the counterpoise of colour and texture in the gardens.

Burlington Cultural Centre
Tuesday-Thursday 12:00-5:00 and
7:00-9:00
Friday 12:00-5:00
Saturday 10:00-5:00
Sunday 1:00-5:00
Closed Mondays
(416) 632-7796

Royal Botanical Gardens
Monday-Friday 10:00-4:00
Saturday & Sunday 10:00-5:00
Extended hours during summer
(416) 527-1158

101

43 JORDAN
Ontario, How Sweet It Is

Niagara is part of Ontario's balmy south, with sunny summers and winter temperatures moderated by two Great Lakes. This climate, along with a mineral-rich soil, makes Niagara ideal for growing tender fruit such as peaches and grapes, and grow they do, all along the Niagara Escarpment from Stoney Creek to Niagara-on-the-Lake. Our summers are too short to miss tasting sweet Niagara during the harvest season from late July to October.

The Niagara Peninsula grows about 15 million grapevines, in about 50 varieties. Some end up for fresh table use, but most in wines. Grapes can also produce juice by the barrelful, as you will find at Wiley Brothers, located at First Street Louth and Eighth Avenue, on the outskirts of St. Catharines.

The Wileys are sixth-generation Niagara fruit growers, specializing in delicious and popular pure fruit juices. Two hundred hectares are planted in grapes, apples, cherries, strawberries and pears. Alert to the growing market for natural foods, Wiley's is beginning to produce organically-grown fruit.

Wiley's has a retail store offering nine types of pure juices and blends (no sugar added) at bargain prices. Wiley's Open House, an extravaganza with slide shows, tastings, plant and vineyard tours, takes place the last two weekends in June. At other times of the year, visitors are welcome for Wiley's lively and informative tours, although an advance phone call lays out the red carpet. Tours include all stages of juice production, from planting (six years before production) through pressing, storage (see refrigerator tanks storing 757,000 litres), aging and bottling.

It's time to head for the open road below, on top of, and through southern Ontario's rocky spine, the grand Niagara Escarpment. Drive south on First Street Louth to Decew and head a short distance east to Mountain Mills Museum. The steep Escarpment was the perfect site for flour and lumber mills. A flour mill was constructed here on Beaverdams Creek in 1872. The mill, rebuilt after a fire in 1895, is now a milling museum surrounded by a park with picturesque waterfall and picnicking sites.

Return north on First Street Louth to Highway 81 (St. Paul Street West) and drive west. Highway 81 goes through the heart of fruitland, with straight rows of vines and fruit trees stretching from the road's edge to the horizon. It is a satisfying view of great order and productivity. The vineyards and orchards are punctuated by nurseries and greenhouses, campgrounds, and charming farm settlements such as Jordan.

The Jordan Museum of the Twenty (local rivers are named for their distance, in miles, from the Niagara River) is worthy of a visit for the tremendous valley view alone, especially good in fall. Relevant to today's trip is an enormous antique fruit press built by the original Mennonite settlers in the area. The schoolhouse portion of the museum includes exhibits on processing the local fruit harvest, via drying and cider-making.

Return to Highway 81. Highway 81 between Vineland and Beamsville is one roadside fruit market after another. If it's time to stretch your legs, there are a few pick-your-own operations. Choose from cherries, red and green grapes, apples, plums, peaches, blackberries, apricots and pears. Bet you can't sample just one!

Beamsville is the home of Montravin Cellars, located on Ontario Street. This small winery produces champagne using old-fashioned, labour-intensive methods. Montravin has scheduled tours on weekdays, or will arrange special tours by appointment; there is a retail store on the premises. Return to the top of the Escarpment and drive west along Regional Road 79 for a bird's-eye view of things.

Head down into Grimsby (along Mountain Street) for two reasons. One, the spectacular view of town and farmland against blue Lake Ontario. Two, to have a meal, if you are not picnicking. Try The Gable Manor at 13 Mountain Street. The Gable serves steak and seafood at lunch and dinner, Tuesday through Sunday. There's even a summer patio. Grimsby is also home to Bistro Benes at 17 Main Street, also closed Mondays.

Head back to Regional Road 79 (also called Ridge Road) and the Beamer Conservation Area. This is one of the best places along the entire Escarpment for feeling like you're lord (or lady) of all you survey. Tidy Grimsby is spread out at your feet, and if you visit in September or October, migrating hawks and eagles are often seen overhead. The nature trails at Beamer are actually part of the famous Bruce Trail which follows the Escarpment from the Bruce Peninsula to Niagara.

Continue on Regional Road 79 until you reach Stoney Creek. Stoney Ridge Cellars are located on Road 79 near Fifty Road. (They will be moving to Highway 8 east of Fifty Road during 1990.) Stoney Ridge Cellars give winery tours and have a retail outlet selling wine, wine-making supplies, and juices for the home winery. As you continue west on Regional Road 79, don't pass the Devil's Punch Bowl without stopping for the magnificent view of the city of Hamilton and Burlington Bay.

Settle the bottles of Wiley juice between the baskets of fruit, so they don't clink all the way home.

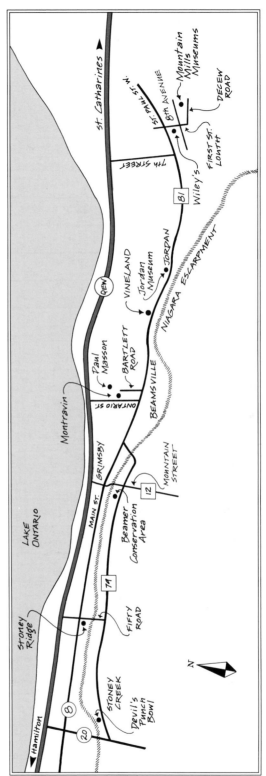

Niagara Escarpment

APPROXIMATE HARVEST TIME FOR FRUIT
IN SOUTHERN ONTARIO

FRUITS	May	June	July	Aug	Sept	Oct
APPLES (summer)				▨ light		
APPLES (fall)					▨ light	■ heavy / ▨ light
BLUEBERRIES (highbush)				■ heavy		
BLUEBERRIES (lowbush)			▨ light	▨ light		
CHERRIES (sweet)			▨ light / ■ heavy			
CHERRIES (tart)			■ heavy			
CURRANTS (black)			▨ light			
CURRANTS (red)			▨ light			
GOOSEBERRIES			▨ light			
GRAPES (wine)					▨ light / ■ heavy	▨ light
PEACHES				▨ light / ■ heavy	▨ light	
PEARS				▨ light	■ heavy / ▨ light	
PLUMS				▨ light	▨ light	
PRUNES					▨ light / ■ heavy / ▨ light	
RASPBERRIES			▨ light / ■ heavy / ▨ light			
STRAWBERRIES		▨ light / ■ heavy	▨ light			

1. ▨ – Light supplies in terms of season and/or availability as a P.Y.O. crop.

2. ■ – Heavy supplies in terms of season and/or availability as a P.Y.O. crop.

3. This chart shows approximate harvest dates for Southern Ontario. For products such as strawberries that grow throughout the province, the season is later in areas outside Southern Ontario.

From the Ontario Ministry of Agriculture and Food

Apple harvest time

Wiley Brothers
Monday-Saturday 8:00-6:00
Sunday 1:00-5:00
(416) 682-0877

Mountain Mills Museum
May-Thanksgiving: Daily 1:00-5:00
Closed Mondays
(416) 937-7210

Stoney Ridge Cellars
June-October: Daily 10:00-5:00
November-May: Saturdays only
Closed Monday year-round
Tours by appointment
(416) 643-4508

Jordan Historical Museum of the Twenty
mid-April to November: Daily 1:00-5:00
(416) 562-5242

Montravin Cellars
(tours) May-October:
Monday-Friday 10:00-4:00
(retail store)
Monday-Friday 9:00-5:00
(416) 563-5313

44 PORT DALHOUSIE
Spend a Day in Port

There's something special about ports and the villages that spring up around them: the smell of water and canvas; the sound of gulls; the charm of brightly painted Victorian buildings; the sense that an adventure is about to begin. Port Dalhousie, near St. Catharines, is no longer a port of great shipping significance, but it retains that distinctive harbourside atmosphere that makes for a great daytrip.

Find Port Dalhousie by exiting the Queen Elizabeth Way at Seventh Street near St. Catharines, heading north to Lakeshore Road, and then east to Main Street in Port Dalhousie. From Niagara, exit at Ontario Street, head north to Lakeport Road, which also leads to downtown Port Dalhousie.

The first thing to do upon entering any port, of course, is to head for the waterfront. There are lots of boats to inspect on both sides of the Dalhousie harbour. Make the effort to drive around to the east side for a look at the postcard-pretty town, with its quayside buildings much as they were a century ago, still peeking out from behind dozens of masts. The entrance to the harbour is guarded by piers and lighthouses that date back 150 years, when the port was the busy terminus of the first three Welland Canals. There's a small park at Lock and Lakeport roads, in the centre of town, commemorating the Welland Canals with a reconstructed wooden lock, parts of a later stone lock, and a tiny clapboard lockmaster's cottage from the 1830s.

Port Dalhousie is ready for shoppers, with many interesting boutiques along Lock Street and Lakeport Road. Fashionable casual wear is available from Magic Mountain Trading Company, South Shore, and Kettle Creek Canvas Company. Diving and windsurfing equipment can be found at Dave's Dive Shop and Ed's Pro Dive. Read 'Em Books is a terrific browse, especially the local travel section. And quality art and gifts are available at several shops, such as The Brick Room, Lighthouse Glass Works and The Rope and Thistle.

The Port Dalhousie of a century and a half ago boasted no less than 17 taverns, always at peak capacity, serving thirsty sailors from around the world. In fact, all the buildings on Lakeport Road east of Lock Street were, at one time or another, taverns or hotels. The quantity may have declined but the quality is probably considerably improved from those early days. Lovely Lakeport Road has two restaurants. Murphy's, on the corner of Lock Street and Lakeport, serves seafood in a nautical setting; even the bar is a converted fishing boat. At the other end of the block is the Port Mansion, probably the area's most photographed building, wearing garlands of twinkling lights each evening. The Mansion was built in 1862 as a hotel, and it is still in the hospitality business, with steaks, seafood and dancing. On Lock Street there's Marie's, a lobster restaurant, and the Lock One Eatery.

Port Dalhousie offers a number of après-lunch activities. The *Garden City* cruise ship carries passengers into Lock 1 of the Welland Canal. The cruises take about two hours and leave the harbour daily at 10AM and 2PM. Popular salmon-fishing charters also operate out of Port Dalhousie; inquire at the tourist information booth near Lakeport Road and Lock Street.

Most daytrippers will head for Lakeside Park. Turn-of-the-century tourists flocked to the beach here, arriving on the regular cruise ship service from Toronto. One of the highlights of Lakeside Park is the antique carousel, with its colourful horses and 120-year-old organ. The price of a ride — one nickel — remains unchanged since its arrival in Port Dalhousie in the 1920s.

Lakeside Park is the home of Canada's smallest jail. The Welland Canal was very busy, with sometimes as many as 2,000 ships passing through in a season. With that many sailors on the loose, a port-side lock-up became essential to keep the peace. This tiny stone building, just around the corner from Port Mansion (convenient location), had two cells, each with its own woodstove; the cost of the fuel came out of the inmates' pockets.

Don't miss the chance to stroll through the peaceful and charming residential areas of Port Dalhousie. Dalhousie Avenue, parallel to Main Street and one block closer to the lake, is particularly interesting. (A guide to historic buildings can be purchased at Read 'Em Books.) If long-distance walking and biking appeal, take advantage of Port Dalhousie's location at the northern end of Merritt Trail, a recreational pathway leading all the way to Port Colborne, at the other end of the canal.

A little further afield are two attractions that draw tourists from around the province. Martindale Pond can be seen by driving south on Lakeport Road, or by driving along Main Street and turning south on Martindale. This was the first rowing course in North America to meet international standards, and the annual Royal Canadian Henley Regatta, held each August, attracts over 2,000 participants. Also on Martindale Road is Stokes Seeds, with a one-hectare trial garden that is brilliant with colour in July and August. Each variety is neatly labelled, so you can start planning next year's flower garden.

It's time to hoist the anchor and sail for home, but no doubt you'll be counting the days until you can set sail for Port Dalhousie again.

Harbour view, Port Dalhousie

Garden City cruises
mid-May to mid-October:
10:00, 2:00 and 7:00
Reservations required for
10:00 and 7:00
(416) 646-2234

Lakeside Park Carousel
early June: Saturday, Sunday &
Holidays 12:00-7:00
mid-June to Labour Day:
Daily 12:00-7:00
(416) 937-7210

Most shops and restaurants
open daily, year-round

45 ST. CATHARINES
Canal Route

Ontario is glued together with engineering works that are considered modern marvels the world over — tunnels, bridges, hydro-electric plants. One of these marvels, the Welland Canal, provides for an unusual and enjoyable daytrip.

The day begins at Port Weller, the northern terminus of the canal and site of Lock 1. Take the Niagara Street North exit off the Queen Elizabeth Way in St. Catharines; Niagara Street ends at Lakeshore Road, and Lock 1 is just to the east.

You can't miss the huge Port Weller Dry Docks, the best place on the canal to study lake freighters and Canadian Navy vessels, as they sit high and dry for repairs. If smaller ships are your pleasure, visit the Port Weller harbour on the eastern side of the canal and inspect the yachts. The western side of the canal is popular for fishing and boat-watching.

Drive south on Canal Road, watching ships pass through Locks 2 and 3 in St. Catharines. Canal Road is lined with good observation and picnic spots. You may be surprised at the large numbers of ship-watchers that congregate along Canal Road to spot ships from as many as 50 countries.

The Welland Canal Viewing Centre is at Lock 3. An elevated platform provides a rare peek into the bridge of gargantuan ocean-going carriers as they descend with the lock. No one can help but be dwarfed by these carriers, measuring the length of two football fields, as they are lifted straight up to the next lock in a matter of ten minutes. Gain respect for the pilots on the giant ships as they pass through locks with centimetres to spare — no wonder so many ships are battle-scarred. The Viewing Centre has a souvenir shop, snack bar and free parking, and there's a posting of when ships can be expected in the lock each day.

At Glendale Avenue, drive west to Merritt Street. Follow signs to number 343, the St. Catharines Historical Museum. (The museum will be relocating to Lock 3 in 1990.) Head for the Welland Canal Gallery for a complete history lesson. The canal of today is actually the fourth Welland Canal. Construction began on the first canal in 1824, a pet project of local hero William Merritt, who appreciated the monetary promise of navigation fees from a Lake Erie-Lake Ontario canal. The modern canal opened in 1932. Each canal has improved on its predecessor by route straightening, city by-passes and increased lock size.

Fascinating historical photographs and newspaper accounts, artifacts and models tell a story of engineering genius, heartbreaking working conditions, and riots among Irish labourers. Through use of photographs and displays, the museum records the rich commercial rewards attracted by the canal, including shipbuilding, railways and other industrial interests.

Upon returning to the canal via Glendale Avenue, don't miss the operation of the lift bridge — it's a real traffic stopper. Follow Canal Road to Locks 4, 5 and 6, the "flight" locks. Ships are raised up the Niagara Escarpment without any intervening stretches of canal, hence the term "flight." (Altogether the canal raises and lowers ships about 99 metres.) Locks 4 through 6 are also known as the "twin" locks, since each lock is actually made of two sections, one for northbound vessels, and the other for south-bound vessels. This is perhaps the best place to ship-watch, since there can be several going through these locks, or waiting their turn, at any time.

On a busy day, as many as two dozen ships may pass through the Welland Canal, in an average transit time of 12 hours. See how many you can distinguish: by national flag, type (bulk carrier, tanker, cement carrier, self-unloader, deep-sea ship), and shipping line (look for the logo on the funnel).

If it is time for a meal, try the Lock 7 Motel and Restaurant. This motel is well known among canal-lovers, who book rooms with a canal view well ahead of each shipping season. The restaurant may not be glamorous, but you are certainly among kindred spirits, who are loaded down with cameras, binoculars and canal trivia.

Lock 7 is the end of scenic Canal Road, and you must turn away from the water for a few minutes. Follow Ormond Street to Highway 58. Westbound, it takes you to Highway 406, and hence to the heart of Welland. Eastbound, a tunnel carries the daytripper *under* the canal, and then south to Welland.

What do you do with an unused canal? Welland has the answer. Part of the fourth canal, rendered obsolete by a Welland Canal by-pass in 1972, is now used for water sports, from water-skiing to swimming. The Recreational Waterway, as it is known, is also the location of a beautiful 1930 lift bridge.

Downtown Welland sports enormous, colourful murals on over a dozen of its buildings. The paintings are not only eye-catching, but provide an interesting lesson on local history such as the building of the Welland Canal.

Welland is a good place for lunch or dinner. The Atlas Pub on Southworth Street is Ontario's first brew pub, and it is also a good place to eat (closed Sunday lunch). In the gourmet line, there's Rinderlin's at 24 Burgar Street. Rinderlin's is open for dinners Monday through Saturday, and lunch on Fridays.

This has been a day to watch the world come to Niagara. Time to say goodbye to Merritt country and head for home.

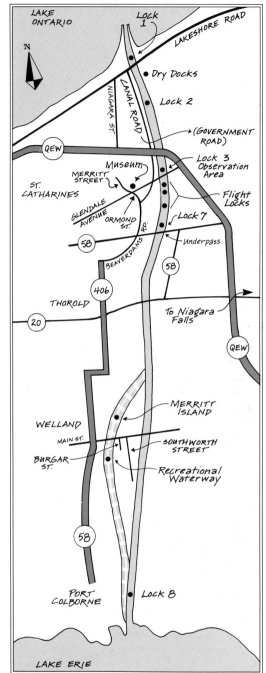

Welland Canal

St. Catharines Historical Museum
Monday-Friday 9:00-5:00
Saturday, Sunday &
Holidays 1:00-5:00
(416) 227-2962

46 NIAGARA-ON-THE-LAKE
The Play's the Thing (But Not Everything)

Niagara-on-the-Lake may be the loveliest, most walkable town in the entire country, but on summer weekends, when throngs of tourists threaten to sink the town with their weight, it very easy to miss Niagara-on-the-Lake's delicate charm. The forewarned daytripper visits mid-week or off-season. Still, even a summer weekend visit can remain civilized, by seeking out the town's beauty spots, many of which are off the beaten track.

The crowning glory of Niagara-on-the-Lake is the Shaw Festival. Even though the large Festival Theatre is nice, seeing a play in the restored Court House or Royal George Theatre is something special. You won't see reruns of plays from the big city, but instead lively productions of Shaw and his contemporaries. It is a very home-grown theatre, with all sets and costumes made by creative and industrious staff. While a trip to Niagara is not complete without a play or two, there's much more here for the daytripper to enjoy.

An effective crowd-avoidance technique is to leave town altogether by taking a cruise on the *Senator*, which is docked near the Niagara-on-the-Lake Sailing Club on Ricardo Street. Sightseeing cruises leave several times daily, and there are dinner cruises Tuesday through Sunday. Moonlight cruises with dancing leave Thursdays, and there's a Sunday brunch cruise as well. The boat sails on the Niagara River south to near the Queenston-Lewiston bridge, giving close-up views of forts George and Niagara. The return trip visits Lake Ontario, with a spectacular horizon of blue punctuated by tall white sails. Look to see the port of origin on the sailboats at the Sailing Club: it's quite an international gathering!

Niagara-on-the-Lake is marvelous for walking. Shady and cool all summer, the side streets are block after block of the most immaculately kept historic homes in Ontario. Only the lush and colourful gardens can compete with the beauty of the houses; they brim with roses, lilies and ivy all season.

Niagara-on-the-Lake

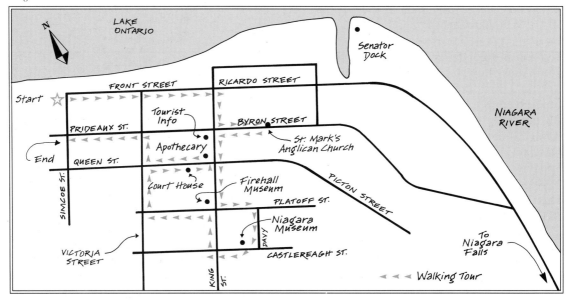

Begin at Front and Simcoe streets. At King walk one block to Prideaux and head east. Prideaux turns into Byron, the location of one of Niagara's many beautiful churches, St. Mark's Anglican Church, built in 1822. Use King Street as a way of crossing busy Picton/Queen Street (the downtown) to the equally picturesque, and even more quiet, south end. Stop at the Tourist Office on King Street to pick up a brochure giving details on the more historic buildings in town. Also on King Street near Queen is the studio and gallery of Trisha Romance, one of Ontario's best-loved painters. Her studio has many studies of local buildings.

Beside the Firehouse on King Street is the small Firehall Museum with a number of antique fire engines and water pumps, all bright red paint and gleaming brass. Walk along to Castlereagh Street, and east one block to the Niagara Historical Museum. This was Ontario's first historical museum, begun in 1806. It has a good collection on the history of Niagara, as well as a delightful herb garden typical of the nineteenth century.

More elegant homes and lush gardens await along Castlereagh and Platoff. Don't miss the section of Platoff from King north to Victoria. Victoria leads back to Queen Street.

Queen Street, with all its crowds, has a few sites of interest. The Court House, built in 1848, was first the seat of county, and then later municipal, governments. It is now a theatre, part of the Shaw Festival. Take a look at Upper Canada's first public library (1800), around the corner in the Court House building.

The Niagara Apothecary at Queen and King streets is the oldest pharmacy in Upper Canada (1866) and is now a museum devoted to the chemists' trade. It contains a wide selection of antique pharmacy implements, such as scales and pill-cutters. Knowledgeable staff help visitors identify some of the more unusual items. Follow your nose to Greaves, where homemade jams and jellies have been produced since 1927. During fruit season, the aroma is intoxicating, and you can sneak a peak at the busy jam-makers in the back room. Don't leave without purchasing jam or jelly in a multitude of flavours, as well as marmalade, chutney or chili sauce.

Niagara-on-the-Lake is one of the best places to walk up an appetite, because the reward is so satisfying. There are many restaurants in town, but the most delightful are those in the hotels and small inns. They give especially good value at lunchtime. The Oban is a personal favourite because of the good food and unparalleled view of the lake. Other fine establishments include the Prince of Wales, Pillar and Post and the Angel Inn. (Reservations are a must during high season at all dining rooms.)

Some people come to town just for the shopping. It is located mainly on Queen Street and nearby sidestreets. There's clothing from casual to glamorous, fine art, collectibles, antiques, Christmas decorations, paper-mâché figures, and designer clothing for kids — heaven for the shopper.

Niagara-on-the-Lake is one of Ontario's true beauty spots, all rose gardens and historic homes. Enjoy it soon.

Shaw Festival Box Office
April-October
(416) 468-2172

Niagara Riverboat Company
(416) 468-4291

Most shops and restaurants
open daily

47 NIAGARA-ON-THE-LAKE
1812 Overture

Residents of Niagara have put their love of country on the line more times than most Canadians, fighting off American invaders before most of the rest of the country was settled. Even though the guns watching over the Niagara River have been silent for over 100 years, the heroes and legends of battle remain alive today in the area around Niagara-on-the-Lake and Queenston. Today's trip takes you back to the War of 1812.

Every war needs a fort, and the Niagara Peninsula has several. Fort George is in Niagara-on-the-Lake. Unlike so many forts of the time, Fort George is made not of stone but of wooden palisades, looking like every child's dream of a frontier fort. No wonder it was so easy for artillery at substantial Fort Niagara, across the Niagara river, to obliterate Fort George. This is actually a twentieth-century reconstruction of the original fort. Only the magazine is original material. Nevertheless, the fort and its costumed soldiers and guides provide a realistic view of life at Fort George.

In the Visitor Centre, dioramas, audio and film material take visitors to the uneasy eve of war. The various participants are introduced: a small but disciplined British army, a brave Canadian militia, Indian allies, and a large but unruly American army.

A self-guided walking tour takes the daytripper through barracks, cookhouse, officers' quarters, and the jail and guardhouse. At the artificer's building, visitors can watch carpenters and blacksmiths fashion tools and repair implements of the day. Activities such as fife-and-drum drills make military life come alive. Climb one of the bastions for a marvellous view of the Niagara-on-the-Lake harbour and daunting Fort Niagara. A telescope provides a soldier's-eye view.

From Fort George head south along the Niagara Parkway to McFarland House, the only house in all of Niagara-on-the-Lake to survive the war. All the rest of the town was burnt to the foundations. McFarland, a wealthy shipbuilder, was himself captured. McFarland House was used as a hospital by both sides during the war, as the house seesawed between British and American possession. It is furnished to the 1800 period, the time of its construction, and costumed guides conduct a brief tour. The tea shop offers luscious fruit in season, among other goodies. The grounds at McFarland House are very popular, with excellent river views and a playground. This is a good picnic spot if you intend to brown bag it today.

Continue south on the Niagara Parkway to Queenston. Queenston was the home of Laura (Ingersoll) Secord, whose heroics during the War of 1812 have endeared her memory to generations of Canadians. Don't miss the imaginative outdoor displays that detail the Secord story: the difficult pioneer life of Loyalists; tending to a wounded husband on the battleground at Queenston Heights; life in a house commandeered by the enemy; and her daring walk from Queenston to St. Catharines to warn the British outpost of a surprise American attack. Her loyalty led to the British victory at Beaverdams.

Although the home was pillaged by invading soldiers, the Laura Secord candy company spared no effort in furnishing it to period. Tours are given daily, and the house includes many items not usually seen: a courting mirror, tobacco box and imported British silverware, for example. A Laura Secord store is on the site.

Queenston was the site of many battles and skirmishes. Many paintings depicting these battles are in the collection at the Samuel E. Weir Library of Art. It is found in Queenston just off the Parkway on Queenston Street. The library has many other works of interest to Canadians.

If time permits, take a tour through Queenston, a pretty, quiet town filled with historic frame homes. It's compact enough for a good walk, or you can do as the locals do and bike it. Bike rentals are available from the South Landing Inn at Kent and Front streets, or at the general store in the centre of town.

For a first-hand look at the area's most infamous battlefield, drive south on the Niagara Parkway to Queenston Heights. The Brock monument marks the site where Brock was buried. A climb to the top (about five storeys) gives a commanding view of the river and steep Escarpment. No wonder the Heights were much coveted by both sides during the war. The park at Queenston Heights has a self-guided tour describing each scene of the battle, and there are organized tours several times daily during the summer.

The main floor of the monument contains exhibits relating to the battle, and Brock's role as hero to the British-Canadian forces. There is an interesting comparison of Brock's monument at Queenston to other relics of the Napoleonic Wars, such as Nelson's monument in London. This puts the War of 1812 into perspective against the larger events in Europe.

The Queenston Heights Restaurant has a breathtaking view of the meandering Niagara River, with a patio perched at the brink of the Escarpment. The food is good all week long, but the Sunday brunch is especially recommended.

The War of 1812 was a major element in the shaping of the Canadian character, and there is no more enjoyable or more scenic way to remember that than in a visit to Niagara.

Fort George
mid-May to June 30:
Daily 9:00-5:00
July 1-Labour Day:
Daily 10:00-6:00
Labour Day-October 31:
Daily 10:00-5:00
November to mid-May by appointment
(416) 468-4257

McFarland House
mid-May to late June:
Daily 1:00-4:30
July-Labour Day:
Daily 11:00-5:00
September & October by appointment
(416) 356-2241

Laura Secord Homestead
late May to mid-October:
Daily 10:00-6:00
(416) 357-4020

Brock's Monument
Victoria Day-Labour Day:
Daily 10:00-6:00
(416) 468-4257

Queenston Heights Restaurant
Daily, year-round
Reservations recommended
(416) 262-4274

48 NIAGARA FALLS
City of Light

Each winter Jack Frost waves his magic wand and transforms the Niagara Falls area into the winter wonderland that Mother Nature designed it to be. The crowds are in retreat, the trees festooned with ice, and the temperatures balmy. This daytrip looks at winter from several different angles, and you are bound to come away refreshed.

The day begins outdoors, cross-country skiing or walking, depending on snow conditions. Three locations offer free skiing. The Whirlpool Golf Course, seven kilometres north of the Falls on the Niagara Parkway, has trails for all levels of skier, with 12 kilometres of trails marked, set and groomed, 10 kilometres unmarked. Facilities include ski rental, coffee shop and restaurant.

There is also the Niagara School of Horticulture, nine kilometres north of the Falls on the Parkway. This peaceful 40-hectare parkland is open for walking and skiing, although there are no groomed trails. An added bonus for naturalists: it is one of the best spots for winter bird-watching in all of Niagara. Check out the feeders for cardinals and chickadees,

and the productive berry bushes for mockingbirds, waxwings and other fruit connoisseurs.

For long-distance devotees, there is the new Niagara Parks Recreational Trail running parallel to the river from Fort Erie to Niagara-on-the-Lake. The trail is hard-surfaced and has been designed for walking, cycling, running and skiing. There are washrooms en route.

Ontario's brisk winter air stimulates the appetite. The Table Rock Restaurant is the best place to view the Falls in winter — as close as you can get to the brink without getting wet. The menu may be uninspired (lasagna, fish and chips), but the food and service are a far sight better than the snack bars offered by most parks commissions. A more extensive menu and better prices are available directly across the street at the Victoria Park Cafeteria. It also offers good views of the Falls, but closes around 5:30PM.

Table Rock is the best spot from which to survey the Falls. The wind whips spray into your face as you brave the elements on the

Festival of Lights

Table Rock overlook. But there are rewards for the intrepid photographer: frozen spray glistens on every tree; an ice bridge forms in the river below; and there are hardly any tourists to leap into your frame at the last moment.

The Niagara Parks people are so obliging to tourists that they even make it possible to experience June in January. The Parks Commission Greenhouse and Plant Conservatory is a stone's throw away, just south of the restaurants — marvelous therapy for the winter blahs. Your soul feasts on a montage of colour, soothing moist air, the quiet drip of a fountain, the fragrance of countless blossoms, the texture of twig and petal.

The early winter visitor is greeted by the famous display of poinsettia, cyclamen and Christmas cactus. Later in winter, the cyclamen — plum, magenta, pink, rose, salmon — are joined by spring favourites such as narcissus, crocus and forsythia, and by southern belles camellia, gardenia and azalea. Young kids are fascinated by the fish pond, which leaves their caretakers free to luxuriate in the spa atmosphere. The Greenhouse and Conservatory are not just a tourist draw; the 135,000 bedding plants that beautify the Niagara Parks are all produced here.

One must return to the realities of winter sooner or later, but it isn't so difficult when the Festival of Lights awaits right outside. The good people of Niagara Falls, apparently afraid that Nature's grandeur isn't enough for us, decorate their parks and streets with a million Christmas lights from late November to mid-February. This is in addition to the nightly illumination of the Falls, which begins at 5:30 during the Festival, and at 7PM otherwise.

The most imaginative light displays are conveniently located for today's daytrip. For a driving tour, concentrate on the Niagara Parkway, a couple of kilometres either side of the Table Rock area. And for walking, don't miss the animated light displays located on Murray Street opposite the Skylon Tower. A troupe of bears hangs out of a bus labelled "Niagara or Bust," a live Santa greets visitors to the North Pole, Thumper and Bambi chase each other, kids cavort in the snow, a loon lands under a full moon — photo opportunities bar none. Don't forget your tripod!

One of the best places to view the winter wonderland after dusk is from the Skylon Tower, which wears a veil of white lights during the Festival (befitting the honeymoon capital of the world). The tower is topped by two dining rooms; the more casual Summit is buffet-style, and the Revolving Dining Room has table service. Both provide extraordinary views of the Festival of Lights, and if you arrive before dusk, the view can extend up to 129 kilometres. There is a charge for the 52-second ride to the top of the tower via an outdoor elevator, but with family rates available, it is well worth the fee.

On this trip we've studied Ontario winter from various points of view: skiing through it until our cheeks are rosy, escaping it entirely in the Conservatory, and observing illuminated snow scenes from over 213 metres up. It's time to shake the snow from our boots and head for home.

Whirlpool Golf Course (skiing)
Daily, depending on conditions
(416) 356-1140

Niagara Parks Greenhouse
Daily, year-round: 9:30-4:30
(extended hours during
Festival of Lights)
(416) 354-1721

Skylon Tower
Daily, year-round: 9:00AM-10:30PM
(416) 356-2651

49 NIAGARA FALLS
Nature's Water Park

One of the biggest tourist fads these days is the water theme park, where people of all ages are tossed about on water slides and in wave pools. Why not spend a day at the original water park, Niagara Falls? A memorable day can be had by seeing the Falls and the great Niagara Gorge in all their natural splendour.

One of the keys to enjoying a trip to Niagara Falls is avoiding the worst of the crowds and traffic. The Parks Commission operates an impressive People Mover bus line which visits major attractions at 15-minute intervals. The People Mover parking lot is on the Niagara Parkway one-and-a-half kilometres south of the Falls. Another tip is to plan your trip slightly off-season, that is, not on weekends in July or August.

The Falls should be observed from a number of vantage points. One of the best known is Table Rock, at the brink of the Horseshoe Falls. The tunnels underneath Table Rock provide an even closer look. The admission price includes lightweight raincoats, which you can keep — a terrific help if capricious Niagara gusts happen to blow the Falls' spray in your direction. The tunnel carries you close to Niagara's thunderous bottom and to two viewing platforms, one at the edge of the Falls and another directly behind. The roar of the Falls echoes in your ears long after you ascend to the surface. Although the tunnels are open until 11PM during the summer, the view is best during daylight.

Probably the most famous attraction at Niagara is the *Maid of the Mist*, operating since 1846. This may be the best ride for your money anywhere, a real-life thrill unequalled by any amusement park. The trip lasts about 30 minutes, travelling to within 91 metres of the Horseshoe Falls, and even closer to the American Falls. The waves at the base of the Falls are tremendously powerful, and the *Maids* (there are several of them) are tossed as the water from four Great Lakes rushes by. Heavy blue raincoats provided at the dock keep you relatively dry, although your coiffure may not survive. Because boats leave every 15 minutes, the lines move well, but a good tip is to try for the last boat of the day, which leaves at 7:15PM during the summer.

If the *Maid of the Mist* trip has piqued your curiosity about the daredevils who have tempted fate and gone over the Falls in a variety of contraptions, the best place to visit is the Daredevil Gallery near the Minolta Tower. This museum has most of the original daredevils' equipment (what remains), newspaper clippings, interviews with survivors, and film footage from inside the last successful vehicle, an aluminum barrel used by Dave Munday in 1985. There's also a terrific, unobstructed view of the entire Falls area from the rooftop.

This may be a good time to break from Falls-viewing and enjoy a good meal. The choice of restaurants is mind-boggling, although finding a really good meal takes a little research. Lundy's Lane is the location of Ye Olde Barn, a ribs-and-chicken eatery popular with locals and tourists. Pardon My Garden, also on Lundy's Lane, has a more adventuresome menu than most Falls restaurants, with lots of seafood and salads. Closer to the action, but with more standard tourist menus, are the Parks Commission's restaurants, the Table Rock and Victoria Park (across the street from the Table Rock and better quality).

Most of us rest content for a glance at the Falls from Table Rock, and then turn away for other amusements. But the Falls themselves are only a part of the myth and legend surrounding Niagara. There's the treacherous rapids and the Whirlpool below the Falls. The closest any sane person would want to get to the rapids is from the observation boardwalk at the Great Gorge Trip, a small

Maid of the Mist

stone building just north of the Falls on the Niagara Parkway. Elevators carry you to river level for a first-hand look — a little drier than the others.

If you'd like a different perspective altogether, there's the Spanish Aero Car, an open cable car that provides a 10-minute trip over the Whirlpool. You can get a bird's-eye view of the Whirlpool, the Falls, Victoria Park, and the Rainbow Bridge from the helicopters that make regular tours of the area. The heliport is located near the Niagara Parkway, just north of the Whirlpool. The Aero Car and helicopters provide unique photo opportunities.

After the action and excitement of the Falls area, there's a less hectic way to study the magnificence of Niagara: the Niagara Glen Nature Area. Drive about seven kilometres north along the Parkway to the Glen; it is located between the Floral Clock and Queenston Heights.

It is a long way down to the bottom of the Niagara Glen. Perhaps it is the stairs that keep the crowds at bay and leaves the four kilometres of hiking trails empty for naturalists to enjoy. Everything here is on a large scale — the Gorge, the trees, and especially the boulders, survivors from when the

Niagara River covered the Glen. This is an excellent place to study the geology of Niagara, and there are informative signs near the top of the stairs. Park naturalists conduct tours during the summer months.

The Niagara River, nature's own water park, will leave you tossed and tousled, but you'll be very pleased that all this excitement is just a daytrip away.

Table Rock Tunnels
Daily, year-round
(416) 354-1551

Maid of the Mist Cruises
May to late October: Daily
(416) 358-0311

Great Gorge Trip
early May to mid-October: Daily
(416) 356-2241

Niagara Spanish Aero Car
March-early November: Daily
(416) 354-5711

50 FORT ERIE
From Fort to Port

The good people of the Niagara Peninsula consider their region to be the cradle of Ontario. Niagara was one of the first areas in the province to be explored and settled by Europeans; it was a primary battlefield during the War of 1812; and many of Ontario's commercial and industrial enterprises have located in Niagara. So it's not surprising that a daytrip to the southern portion of the Niagara Peninsula can touch on all the major elements of Ontario's development.

Begin the day in Fort Erie, at the southern end of the Queen Elizabeth Way. Follow signs to Old Fort Erie, located at the head of the Niagara River.

Visitors to the fort are immersed in military life on the frontier of Upper Canada during the early nineteenth century. During the summer, authentically attired soldiers re-enact many facets of army life: musket and cannon drills, marching, and complaining. Tours are conducted each hour and feature lively descriptions of the soldier's miserable life: crowded barracks, continual marching drills, and the threat of flogging. A barracks

building houses a military museum displaying period uniforms, weapons, and miscellaneous items discovered during archaeological digs at the fort.

Although not strictly within the topic of Niagara history, Fort Erie is the location of another first-rate attraction, Mildred M. Mahoney Dolls' House Museum. It is located at 657 Niagara Boulevard, about one kilometre north of the Peace Bridge. Nothing could be further removed from the bloody battles of 1814 than this sedate museum; and if you think that dolls' houses and miniatures are not for you, the Mahoney Museum will change your mind.

The museum is two large floors of antique dolls' houses, some dating back two centuries. They are crammed with miniature furnishings of every description — original oil paintings, Limoges china, needlepoint carpets and cherrywood dining suites. This is a good opportunity to study domestic architecture from across Europe, Japan and North America, and interior design through the ages, as each house is authentic and complete in every possible detail. This is

Historic Fort Erie

not a "hands-on" museum, so young children may be happier elsewhere.

Next, head for Port Colborne by driving along Highway 3. Port Colborne has many sites of interest and provides a different view of Niagara's busy history. The Port Colborne Historical and Marine Museum is located on King Street, south of Main Street (Highway 3). It comprises about a half-dozen buildings dating to the pioneer era, as well as the bridge from a lake tug.

Exhibits describe the history of the Welland Canal. Although settlement came early to this area, prosperity arrived with the canal during the 1830s, when Port Colborne became a ship-trade town, supplying ships and crews with essential supplies, food and lodging. The Welland Canal had this same effect on many other communities it traversed, and it radically changed the face of Niagara. Those days are relived through an excellent assembly of historic photographs.

To see the canal first-hand, head for the Welland Canal Lock 8 Observation Area, also known as the "jackknife bridge" area (north on King, east on Main). Lock 8 is one of the longest locks in the world, and this is a very pleasant park for watching ships. Fine dining with a lock view can be found at popular Stonebridge Island House on Main Street by the canal; there's a patio for boat-watching during fair weather. Other good eateries in the area include Barette's Bistro, at 115 Main Street West, and at 265 Main Street West, The Home of 2 Chefs.

Continue a canal-side tour by driving south on King Street and east on Clarence. The Clarence Street lift bridge rises 37 metres in the air to allow ships passage into the canal. If the bridge is being raised, stop to watch the show; and if the bridge is down, take advantage of the view it provides of previous Welland Canals.

South of Clarence is West Street, home to a number of shops in recycled nineteenth-century canal-side hotels and stores. They sell marine wear, boating accessories and crafts. You can continue driving south to

Lake Erie, where there are two marinas offering boat rentals, launching, gas, and everything else you need. Lakeview and Harbourview parks are good for a stroll. Feel like a swim? Head for Nickel Beach by driving back to Clarence, crossing the Welland Canal, and heading south to the lakeshore again.

Port Colborne was also a cottage town, and the museum has a fascinating description of the genteel Southern families from Tennessee who lived along Tennessee Avenue each summer around the turn of the century. To reach Tennessee Avenue from the museum, drive south on King Street to Sugarloaf, then west to the stone gates of Tennessee Avenue. Number 19 Tennessee Avenue is the original casino for the Humberstone Summer Resort Company.

From fort to port, this has been the story of life on the Niagara frontier, where Upper Canada began.

Historic Fort Erie
(tentative)
mid-May to Labour Day:
Daily 10:30-5:00
(416) 871-0540

Mildred Mahoney
Dolls' House Museum
May 1-December:
Daily 10:00-4:00
(416) 871-5833

Port Colborne Historical and
Marine Museum
May-December:
Tuesday-Sunday 12:00-5:00
Monday by appointment
(416) 834-7604

BIBLIOGRAPHY

Information on tourist attractions came from a multitude of sources. Government publications and brochures printed by public and private facilities are too numerous to mention, but the following published sources deserve recognition.

Brown, Ron. Backroads of Ontario. Edmonton: Hurtig, 1984.

Cantor, George. The Great Lakes Guidebook. Lakes Erie and Ontario. Ann Arbor: University of Michigan, 1978.

Chandler, Margaret Ross. The Great Little Country Inns of Southern Ontario. Toronto: Deneau, 1989.

Eedy, Lorne. "Take the Eedy Walk Through Town." Supplement to the St. Marys Journal-Argus. May 18, 1988.

Fremes, Marvin. Historic Inns of Ontario. Toronto: Deneau.

Gillham, Skip, and Don Revell. The Welland Canal: A Visitor's Guide. St. Catharines: Vanwell, 1986.

Goodwin, Clive E. A Bird-Finding Guide to Ontario. Toronto: University of Toronto, 1982.

Hardy, Anne, editor. Where to Eat in Canada. Ottawa: Oberon, 1988.

Howes, Hylda, editor. Heritage Buildings of Norfolk. Erin: The Boston Mills Press.

Judd, W.W., and J. Murray Speirs. A Naturalists's Guide to Ontario. Toronto: University of Toronto, 1964.

Lutman, John H. The Historic Heart of London. London: London Public Library Board, 1988.

Miner, Manly R. Jack Miner. Unpublished book.

Murphy, Larry. Thomas Keefer. Don Mills: Fitzhenry and Whiteside, 1977.

Riendeau, Roger. An Enduring Heritage. Black Contributions to Early Ontario. Toronto: Dundurn, 1984.

Scharfenberg, Doris. The Long Blue Edge of Ontario: A Vacation Guide to Canada's Great Lakes Coasts. Grand Rapids: Eerdman, 1984.

Snowden, Annette. Discover Southern Ontario. Toronto: Irwin, 1985.

Wilson, L.W., and L.R. Pfaff. Early St. Marys. Erin: The Boston Mills Press, 1981.